PENGUIN
SPECIALS

Penguin Specials fill a gap. Written by some of today's most exciting and insightful writers, they are short enough to be read in a single sitting – when you're stuck on a train; in your lunch hour; between dinner and bedtime. Specials can provide a thought-provoking opinion, a primer to bring you up to date, or a striking piece of fiction. They are concise, original and affordable.

To browse digital and print Penguin Specials titles, please refer to **penguin.com.au/penguinspecials**

# LOWY INSTITUTE

The Lowy Institute is an independent, nonpartisan international policy think tank. The Institute provides high-quality research and distinctive perspectives on the issues and trends shaping Australia's role in the world. The Lowy Institute Papers are peer-reviewed essays and research papers on key international issues affecting Australia and the world.

For a discussion on *Best Laid Plans*, visit the Lowy Institute's daily commentary and analysis site, *The Interpreter*: **lowyinstitute.org/the-interpreter/debate/best-laid-plans**

The election victory of Myanmar's National League for Democracy (NLD) in 2015 ushered in a period of dramatic economic reform. These reforms, flawed, incomplete, and ultimately crushed by the 2021 coup that returned Myanmar to military rule, aimed not just to turn around the country's dire economy, but also to lay the foundations for a more peaceful and democratic state.

This small book offers a unique first-hand account of Myanmar's efforts at economic reform under the NLD government and its leader, Daw Aung San Suu Kyi. Written by one of her key economic advisers, who was imprisoned alongside her in the wake of the coup, the book explores the government's plans, the resistance these inspired, and the events that brought this brief reform era to an end.

LOWY INSTITUTE

# Best Laid Plans: The Inside Story of Reform in Aung San Suu Kyi's Myanmar

## A LOWY INSTITUTE PAPER

## SEAN TURNELL

PENGUIN BOOKS

UK | USA | Canada | Ireland | Australia
India | New Zealand | South Africa | China

Penguin Books is part of the Penguin Random House group of companies
whose addresses can be found at global.penguinrandomhouse.com

Penguin
Random House
Australia

First published by Penguin Books, 2024

Cover image by *The Asahi Shimbun* via Getty Images
Typeset by Midland Typesetters, Australia

Printed and bound in Australia by Griffin Press, an accredited
ISO AS/NZS 14001 Environmental Management Systems printer

A catalogue record for this
book is available from the
National Library of Australia

ISBN 978 1 76134 677 4

penguin.com.au

MIX
Paper | Supporting
responsible forestry
FSC® C018684

# CONTENTS

*The best laid plans of mice and men*
*Go oft awry,*
*And leave us nothing but grief and pain,*
*For promised joy.*

Robert Burns, *To a Mouse* (English trans), 1785

*Anyone can turn a fish into fish soup, but it is much*
*harder to turn fish soup into a fish.*

Michael Zantovsky, *Havel: A Life,* 2014

# CHAPTER ONE

# The best laid plans

'The Myanmar Sustainable Development Plan . . . is founded upon the objective of giving coherence to the policies and institutions necessary to achieve genuine, inclusive, and transformational economic growth.'

Daw Aung San Suu Kyi,
State Counsellor of the Union of Myanmar, 2018

From 2016 to 2021, Myanmar underwent a period of profound economic reform. Driven by the National League for Democracy (NLD) government of Daw Aung San Suu Kyi, this reform program aimed to lay the economic foundations for liberal democracy, as well as reverse Myanmar's five-decade retrenchment into oppression, disorder, and poverty. Hitherto an outlier among the economic growth that has otherwise characterised the region, by 2021 Myanmar seemed at last to be on the cusp of following its fast-growing peers and neighbours.

As 'Special Economic Consultant' to Daw Aung San Suu Kyi, I was both a witness to and participant in this bold experiment.[1] Lest this suggest otherwise, however, it is important to stress right from the get-go that the intellectual forces behind the economic reforms of this era were overwhelmingly local in source and inspiration. Led by a small cohort of relatively young and unambiguously brave deputy ministers, Myanmar's economic reforms were ideologically centrist within the broad frame of liberal democratic capitalism. Traces of the Washington Consensus – that standard set of market-oriented policy recommendations for developing countries promoted by the World Bank, International Monetary Fund, and US Treasury – were certainly visible, but arguably no more so than policies yielded from the success of Myanmar's neighbours.[2] Pragmatic but principled, Myanmar's economic reformers knew that implementation would be more important than inspiration.

Time was in short supply for Myanmar's elected civilian government and its reform-minded advisers, as was authority. Authority over a bureaucracy designed decades ago to serve a military-socialist state – top-down, sclerotic, and decidedly unfit for purpose. And authority over Myanmar's military, particularly its purse, its personnel, and its actions.

Meandering, with intent, would be the reformers' order of business. Ducking and weaving, finding progress in the cracks. As the great philosopher of economic development Albert Hirschman once put it, 'progress can at times meander strangely through many peripheral areas before it is able to dislodge backwardness from the central positions . . .'[3]

The coup that returned Myanmar to the rule of a military junta in February 2021 brought about an end to economic reform, and with it the prospects of another generation of young Burmese escaping the poverty and despair that military rule had bestowed upon their parents and grandparents. To the reformers themselves, who throughout this book I will often simply refer to as 'we', the coup brought about immediate suffering – at best dismissal, usually imprisonment, torture, sometimes exile, even death. Denied any influence over an economic catastrophe their talent might have averted, and locked away from the world, the story of what Myanmar's reformers attempted has yet to be told. It is my intention in this book to at least partially remedy this omission, as best I can.

As a participant in the story that follows, I bring certain advantages and disadvantages to the role of commentator. On the one hand, I know much about what happened behind the scenes. This is important in the context of Myanmar, where much was, and remains, opaque. The phrase 'You had to be there' came readily to mind as I contemplated so many events here, good and bad. On the other hand, I confess I am not an entirely objective observer, and nor did I see everything that went on. I try hard in these pages to be fair, and I believe I bring a critical eye even to policies and programs that I championed. Nevertheless, as my great predecessor in Myanmar Louis Walinsky once wrote in his own account of economic reform in the 1950s, 'on this score . . . the reader is entitled to approach the work with some doubt.'[4]

The reader will also see that this book is concerned with Myanmar's *economic* reform journey, and not that of its political trajectory more broadly. Of course, economics and politics can never really be separated, so politics shares the stage throughout. But economic reform, especially in its financial and institutional aspects, is very much my focus. This concentration reflects whatever expertise I brought, the principal areas in which I worked, as well as my conviction that Myanmar's financial dysfunctions were central to its broader miasma. In doing so, I trust I'm not engaging in excessive economic determinism, but simply recognising a truth with long legs in experience: a healthy economy is not a sufficient condition for a healthy society, but it sure is a necessary one.

Beyond some of the major participants, there is an under-representation of Burmese *names* in this book. This is deliberate, and tragic. This book is the story of countless people in Myanmar who, day by day, toiled to deliver the reforms described, and to create the democracy for which they had sacrificed much. Alas, my identifying – my rightful celebration – of such inspiring people will do them no favour. Indeed, it will bring them retribution from the regime that now rules over them, and which has taken Myanmar into a new darkness. Nameless they are for the moment, forgotten they are not.

*

The opening line of my 2009 book on Myanmar's monetary and banking history contains a declaration that Burma, as the country was then known, had begun the 20th century as the richest country in Southeast Asia, and entered the 21st as the poorest.[5] Of course, GDP numbers are notoriously unreliable, not least in Myanmar, but there is little doubt about this trajectory. Throughout the 20th century, Myanmar's economy, especially as it was lived by the ordinary person, slid relentlessly down the league tables of national wellbeing.[6]

The cause of this descent was clear to all but the most obdurate of military-regime apologists. It was politics pure and simple. But not just politics of the pedestrian, prosaic variety, the sort that disappoints daily. No, this was politics at the ragged edge; politics of the sort practised only by regimes cursed to be without checks and balances. Politics, shorn of euphemism and jargon, of the mad and bad.

For followers of Myanmar, the story of the country's economic dystopia is a familiar one, but it is a tale that should not be forgotten, not least to provide context to the events covered in this book: independence from the British Empire in 1948, a mildly socialist parliamentary democracy for a decade or so, some missteps, and a familiar misplaced faith in economic planning. Yet in this era, economic foundations were laid in Myanmar that would have seen it adequately placed to benefit when Southeast Asia's other economies started to roar.

Alas, Myanmar did not become like its neighbours. In 1962, a military coup dragged the country into some of the worst excesses of state control seen anywhere. Under the regime's slogan of the 'Burma road to socialism', enterprises large and small were nationalised and farmers' output expropriated while the state became little more than a vehicle for patronage, corruption, and erratic policymaking on an epic scale. To outsiders, this was only occasionally noticed, as when, in 1970, orders were issued that Myanmar's right-hand drive cars henceforth be driven on the right-hand side of the road, with all the attendant mayhem and traffic-related deaths. Then there were currency note demonetisations, notably in 1987, which temporarily substituted the decimal system for one based on the number nine, regarded as auspicious for the country's then dictator, General Ne Win. All darkly comic in its way, unless one had to live under it.

Matters came to a head in 1988, when Myanmar was convulsed by demonstrations against the ruling military by a people who had had enough. As was characteristic, then and later, the regime responded with deadly force. Thousands were killed, many more imprisoned, while a substantial cohort of Myanmar's youth – among them the country's best and brightest – fled abroad. In 1990, in a bizarre episode of hubris, Myanmar's rulers conceded to present themselves to an election. They lost in a landslide to the newly formed National League for

Democracy (NLD) and its charismatic leader, Daw Aung San Suu Kyi. The military then stopped pretending. The results of the election were annulled. New oppression followed. Daw Aung San Suu Kyi and most of her fellow NLD members were arrested and incarcerated. Daw Suu, as I always called her, would be imprisoned for most of the following two decades, during which time she was awarded the Nobel Peace Prize (1991).

Myanmar stagnated anew. Twenty years passed before a cohort of military leaders emerged who, though neither liberal nor democratic, began to understand the depths to which Myanmar's economy had sunk. Some recognised that reforms were needed, others understood that the *appearance* of change was at least necessary. In 2008, a new constitution was drawn up, from which would come the 'semi-military' government of President Thein Sein. The military would continue to hold all critical powers: complete discretion over their own budget and total control over the Ministry of Home Affairs, the security services, the police, and border affairs. The Commander-in-Chief of the armed forces also held a variety of reserve powers. He (and it could not be imagined it would not be a 'he') could intervene in the governing of the country at any time, declare a state of emergency, and take charge. There were some supposed safeguards against misuse of these powers, but they were not perceived to matter and, when it came to the test, they did not.

Nevertheless, from 2010 a program of economic reform that accompanied these political moves seemed to flourish. For a while. Much of this was superficial, the appearance of reform, often for international consumption. It was what people in Myanmar call '*Shwe Ye Same*'.[7] Form substituted for function; 'looks like' for 'does'.[8]

Yet one must not be *too* churlish about this period. Superficial or not, the depths to which Myanmar had sunk meant that for a while even mild changes had an impact. From 2010, economic growth in Myanmar rose steeply off its low base, before just about reaching the point where broader change to the country's *political* economy would be necessary to drive further growth. Technocratic change had reached its limit. Elections were scheduled for 2015, with the quasi-military government expecting to win. Enough change, or so they thought, to appease the people and an international community that was not demanding much.

Unfortunately for Thein Sein and his cohort, the people of Myanmar wanted more. Once again, the military and its proxies lost the elections in a land-slide. Aung San Suu Kyi and the NLD won nearly

80 per cent of the contested parliamentary seats.[9] The 2008 Constitution, however, dictated that Suu Kyi could not be president. Her husband had been a British citizen, as were her two sons. According to Article 59(f), the president must be someone who 'shall he himself [sic], one of the parents, the spouse, one of the legitimate children or their spouses not owe allegiance to a foreign power, not be subject of a foreign power or citizen of a foreign country'.[10] No matter. Her brilliant legal adviser, U Ko Ni, who former officers of Myanmar's military would assassinate in January 2017, found a loophole in the constitution, a legal space in which to create a role 'above' the president. As 'State Counsellor', Suu Kyi assumed the effective leadership of Myanmar's NLD government when it was sworn in, in March 2016.

## THE MYANMAR SUSTAINABLE DEVELOPMENT PLAN

The NLD had not spent decades in the wilderness, with many of its members in prison, to settle for an economic program that dealt with mere superficialities when it finally got into office. Accordingly, but after something of a slow start as it grappled with the change-resistant civil service, it began to roll out reforms of increasing boldness. These were given coherence early in 2018 when they were published together under the moniker of the 'Myanmar Sustainable Development Plan' (MSDP).[11]

The MSDP was the four-letter abbreviation that dominated economic discussion in Myanmar in the NLD era. The product of the fertile minds of three of Myanmar's most committed reformers, all of deputy minister rank – U Winston Set Aung, U Bo Bo Nge, and U Min Ye Paing Hein – the MSDP articulated five goals, beneath which was a dizzying array of action plans, targeted outcomes, designated actors, and assessment metrics. These were not prescriptive – central planning of the old form was not on the table – but they gave some indication of where the reformers saw the country going, and how to get there.

Creating an economy safe for peace and democracy was the first goal of the MSDP, which contained in its introduction the declaration that:

Foundational to all strategies and Action Plans noted within this MSDP is recognition of the economic dividends yielded from being a democracy. An end in itself and, as such, needing no other justification, it is the case that being a democracy brings the application to Myanmar the most powerful engine of economic growth known to human history. A system based on individual rights and freedoms, democracy and its accompanying institutions aligns incentives, allows spontaneous solutions to problems, promotes technological advancement and the delivery of public services according to demand, and expands choice and opportunity. In short, democracy and a focus on individual rights and the rule of law are simultaneously the ends of policy, and the vehicles through which Myanmar may escape poverty and achieve the prosperity our people deserve.

All of this was consistent with the contemporary writings of such development thinkers as William Easterly, Daron Acemoglu, and James Robinson, whose works were influential among Myanmar's reformers.[12] Acemoglu and Robinson's book, *Why Nations Fail,* was ubiquitous, and was a favourite present given to Aung San Suu Kyi by foreign visitors. So much so that she once complained to me, early in the government's term, 'Why do all these people think I need a book telling me how nations fail? I want to know how they succeed.'

A section in the MSDP on the importance of peace was more distinctive to the Myanmar context.[13] Noting the 'more than 60 years of debilitating conflict' the country had suffered, the MSDP went on to say that 'unless a durable nation-wide peace is achieved, it will be considerably more difficult to ensure that the development efforts described throughout the MSDP can truly reach those made most vulnerable due to conflict.' Peace was thus the 'priority of priorities', which would partly depend upon equitable socio-economic development. As the MSDP put it, 'peace cannot be sustained without inclusive development' and vice versa. Special attention was also given to the need for Myanmar to establish functional federalism, outlining how equalisation payments and fiscal transfers might be employed to unite the country's states and regions.

The second goal of the MSDP was about steadying Myanmar's chronically unstable macroeconomy. To this end, a number of policies were advanced, all within the boundaries of sound policymaking more or less everywhere where prosperity is apparent, including among Myanmar's neighbours. There were commitments to 'float' Myanmar's currency, the *kyat;* to eliminate central bank financing of the government (aka, 'printing money'); to create a viable tax system, including by introducing a Value Added Tax; to construct a government debt market as the foundation of new capital markets; and to reform Myanmar's state-owned enterprises or privatise them where appropriate.

Central bank independence – granting it autonomy to achieve price and currency stability – was another recommendation of the MSDP. Of course, in rich countries the notion that a central bank should be independent of government is uncontroversial, if not de rigueur. For developing countries, however, the issue is more divisive. On the one hand, such independence is demonstrably the best single undertaking to deliver price and monetary stability. On the other, in developing countries central banks are often tasked with other responsibilities. Some of these are unfortunate – funding the government through money-printing; being the source of favour and largesse – while others are more justifiable, such as creating institutions needed for financial sector growth. In the end, we reformers came down in favour of independence; Myanmar's monetary history was just too volatile to muck around with half measures. Nevertheless, as per St Augustine, we wanted to be virtuous, but not just yet. The Central Bank of Myanmar (CBM) was not, at the start of the NLD administration, fit for independence. Poorly staffed, badly led, and under-resourced, it needed a thorough clean-up, restructure, and reinvigoration if it was going to fulfil anything other than its historical role as a tame dispensary for military spending.

Meanwhile, the MSDP put some firm numbers on its fiscal objectives, committing to keep any budget deficits to within five per cent of GDP.

The MSDP was clear (the third goal) that transformational economic growth in Myanmar would be led by the private sector. But how to support private enterprise? The most important way was for government, so overbearing for much of Myanmar's history, to simply get out of the way. Under the MSDP came 70 or so liberalising measures, including freeing farmers from government direction on 'what, how, and when' to produce; allowing farmers complete freedom in selling their product, ending forced procurement and state-dictated prices; and giving farmers unfettered access to international markets, allowing them to export any or all of their produce.

The liberalising instinct extended beyond agriculture. Most limits on foreign direct investment (FDI) were eliminated. Certain restrictions remained in telecommunications and sectors overtly concerned with national security, but an open door to FDI was the default assumption. According to the MSDP, investment policies were to be revised 'with the aim of ensuring a level playing field for all investors, and to create in Myanmar a favourable, predictable and friendly investment climate.' As with farmers, private enterprises were given complete freedom in what and how they produced, who they could sell to and contract with, and at what prices. Unremarkable rights in most countries, for sure, but in Myanmar such freedoms amounted to a revolution.

Greater freedoms were also granted on the import side. Removed were any restrictions on the buying of foreign exchange for import purposes, while the myriad protective tariffs Myanmar had employed were gradually rationalised. Instead, a universal, flat, and low 'revenue tariff' would be introduced to raise funds, not to be a vehicle for protectionism. Myanmar's exporters and importers had long had to deal with suffocating layers of red tape. This was a useful and time-honoured means for official graft but a substantial handicap to any thought of applying to Myanmar the export-led growth model so successfully employed by the Asian 'tiger' economies. The MSDP set out an array of action plans to eliminate as much of this as possible while making transparent all the procedures traders had to go through. Establishing a one-stop shop for customs and other procedures was therefore a priority, based on successful precedents within Myanmar's existing special economic zones.[14]

Of course, there were positive actions the state could take to promote private sector activity, beyond simply freeing it up. None of this involved government 'picking winners', but it did involve reforms to bring greater investor certainty and lower costs. Foremost were assurances with respect to property rights. Land, especially that allocated to agriculture, had traditionally been exclusively owned by the state, with farmers granted only *use* rights. Creating fully private ownership across all forms of land title was an important long-term goal of the MSDP. In a related but broader objective, the MSDP asserted the importance of the rule of law in Myanmar and independent courts. Of course, the ambition on this front extended well beyond simply economics, and a tough and uncertain struggle was assured.

Other measures of private sector support included commitments on delivering better infrastructure – primarily electricity, roads, bridges, and ports. The MSDP acknowledged this would be costly and place at risk the five per cent budget deficit commitment. To get around this, and to give Myanmar the quality infrastructure it needed, a range of mechanisms made an appearance in the MSDP, from the continued promotion of special economic zones to the first real private-public partnerships. Of course, private finance would not be available for infrastructure projects that, even if they yielded clear socioeconomic returns, might not be profitable. For those projects, the MSDP envisaged straightforward financing from the government budget, as well as official foreign development assistance to the extent prudent.

Accessing sufficient and reliable electricity was one of the greatest challenges facing private enterprise in Myanmar. Myanmar's electricity grid was outdated and poorly maintained, and many people (especially in rural areas) were not connected to it.[15] Turning this around was a central plank of government support for the private sector in Myanmar, both in terms of committed budget allocations, and the profile given to cooperation with development partners on the issue (unstated in the MSDP, but we had the World Bank primarily in mind). The MSDP also directed government attention to the likely availability of financing for renewable energy, primarily solar. The framers of the MSDP thought Myanmar ripe for a much 'greener' approach to power generation.

Improving governance within Myanmar's sluggish civil service was a necessary complement to facilitating the private sector. Understood to be a Herculean task across many generations, the MSDP recommended measures designed to bring about transparency and accountability, coupled with retrenching underperforming personnel. Gender and racial equalities of opportunity were declared as cross-cutting objectives across all MSDP policies, but it was in public sector employment that the civilian government would be able to bring about change most quickly. It was understood from the start that there would be great resistance to such reforms from some incumbent staff.

Access to capital had been a binding constraint on Myanmar's private sector. The financial sector reforms to remedy this were substantial, and generated much opposition, as will be discussed in the next chapter.

The fourth goal of the MSDP was concerned with building human capital through improvements in Myanmar's health and education systems. These had long taken a back seat to resourcing the military, but free primary education and healthcare were determined to be basic rights, which meant greater financial and other resources had to be allocated to each. Both would also be made accessible regardless of gender, ethnicity, or any other basis for differential treatment.

Replacing the 'rote learning' approach that had hitherto been the dominant teaching method, the MSDP contained a commitment to introducing a curriculum emphasising 21st-century skills and concepts, including sustainable development, human rights, gender equality, global citizenship, and cultural diversity. Technical, vocational education and training (TVET) was strongly advocated by the MSDP to serve the emergence of manufacturing and to avoid the inequalities present in many developing countries of an elite tertiary sector and inadequate education for everyone else.

On the health front, the first objective of the MSDP was to increase spending across the board, funded by the fiscal measures already noted and, in the longer run, the diversion of financial resources allocated to the military. Such extra spending was needed across every component of the health sector, but all to meet the goal of being able to provide a defined and universal 'basic health package'.[16] Progress was not expected to be rapid.

Social security was almost non-existent in Myanmar at the outset of the NLD government, and progress towards a basic social safety net was not expected to be brisk under it. However, the MSDP contained a number of provisions to lead to one, including unconditional cash transfers to pregnant women, an expanded school food program, as well as incapacity benefits and increased payments to the very old (Myanmar did not have a non-contributory pension scheme for the general population below 90 years of age).

Environmental protection and better resource management were prominent concerns for the

NLD, and commitments on this front made up the fifth goal of the MSDP. The issues were related, of course – resource extraction, wasteful fossil fuel subsidies, illegal logging, destruction of habitats, poaching and trafficking of protected flora and fauna – all touching upon the unsustainability of too many damaging practices in Myanmar, and boundless economic inefficiencies. Myanmar's great alluvial rivers (the Irrawaddy, Salween, Sittaung, and Chindwin) provided the country with fresh water at volumes far in excess of the rest of Asia, but this extraordinary resource, critical in making the Ayeyarwady Delta one of the most naturally fertile rice-growing regions in the world, was fast being polluted and squandered. Reversing this trend was a key objective of the MSDP and an identified area for international cooperation.

The necessity for new mining laws and rules was acknowledged in the MSDP, to protect affected communities (most often in ethnic minority areas) and the environment, as well as to allow much greater transparency in revenue flows.[17] The idea that Myanmar had been a victim of a 'resource curse' was often cited by activists, and to this end the MSDP recommended the acceleration of Myanmar's accession to the Extractive Industries Transparency Initiative (EITI) and ultimately the establishment of a sovereign wealth fund for resource and energy revenues.

The MSDP was launched with great fanfare in 2018 in the capital, Naypyitaw. It was greeted favourably by pretty much everyone. Truth was, part of this was relief that it was finally out, following much delay within the Ministry of Planning and Finance. According to the in-country head of the World Bank, 'the MSDP provides the framework to realize [Myanmar's] potential by building human and physical capital and by harnessing this nation's innovative and creative power, including by mobilizing a dynamic private sector.'[18] According to another commentator, it marked the emergence of 'Suukyinomics'.[19] The label did not stick.

## A LITTLE HELP FROM FRIENDS

For the first couple of years of the NLD government, Myanmar was very much flavour of the month in international development circles. A veritable gold-rush of bilateral and multilateral development agencies, together with their camp followers, poured in, repeating a phenomenon that had occurred in the wake of the first of the Thein Sein reforms (from about 2013) and to potentially the same deleterious effects. Many of these agencies quickly found the environment too tough, and became just one among many NATO ('no action, talk only') visitors. In order to make something out of the rush, and to limit 'NATO' as much as possible, one of the first acts of Myanmar's reformers was to establish the Development Assistance Coordination Unit, which was all about getting as much benefit for Myanmar as possible from donors while trying to keep everyone concerned from engaging in turf wars or just tripping over themselves.

*

The World Bank was the most important multilateral financial institution operating in Myanmar. With programs and policy advice across just about every conceivable area of the economy and society, its efforts were especially conspicuous in energy (restoring and expanding Myanmar's electricity generating capacity, including by embracing renewables), agriculture, the financial sector, education, and health. Finally, the Bank was a font of good policy advice courtesy of a team of exceptionally skilled and dedicated in-house and local economists.

The International Monetary Fund (IMF) had a small presence in Myanmar. But, with highly effective country directors in location throughout the

NLD years, it played an outsize role analytically and in policy influence.

Among bilateral development partners, the most useful in my judgement were the United States, the United Kingdom, and Australia. As with the IMF and World Bank, much of this was serendipitous. The economic and aid teams from these three countries were unusually well-informed, empowered to make decisions, sympathetic to the reform cause, and conspicuously energetic. In the case of the United States, much of the support came in the form of macroeconomic and monetary advice, as well as a comprehensive United States Agency for International Development (USAID) program to support policy and institutions to facilitate the growth of the formal private sector.

In practice, USAID support largely came via subcontracted private firms, elsewhere disparaged in development discourse as 'beltway bandits' in reference to the location of their head offices, usually in Washington, D.C. and its surrounds. Such characterisations were, in my view, misplaced. The greater flexibility offered by these firms, especially in securing expertise quickly and without fuss, gave reason to recommend the model.[20]

The United Kingdom was a bulwark of support for Myanmar's reforms. As with the United States, this support was multi-faceted but, reflecting London's unique role as an international financial centre, assistance on monetary, banking, and trade policy was a speciality. Our efforts at trying to bring Myanmar into compliance with the Anti-Money Laundering and Counter-Terrorism Financing standards of the Financial Action Task Force (FATF), for instance, were effectively bankrolled by the United Kingdom, while the Bank of England was also a generous source of advice and connections to global capital markets. Another special attribute for which our British partners were rightly proud was the deliberate flexibility and speed applied to their assistance funds, making the United Kingdom the effective 'paramedics' of development partners.

Australia's aid to Myanmar concentrated on education, but as with their American and British counterparts, Australia was a steady source of expertise in a range of economic areas, from public sector reform to infrastructure financing. And, of course, my own position as adviser to Daw Aung San Suu Kyi and the NLD government was the product of Australian aid. Although often a parochial conceit, in my opinion Australia really did 'punch above its weight' in Myanmar. As with the United States and the United Kingdom, this was perhaps less a function of the dollar sign attached to Australia's contributions and more a result of the imagination and energy of the team on the ground.[21]

The European Union also had a large presence in Myanmar during the reform period. Many of its programs, especially in public financial management of the type that brought fellow Aussie Leigh Mitchell to Myanmar as an adviser to the Ministry of Planning and Finance, made quiet but real progress. It might be jejune to say, but other initiatives suffered from the European Union's many and steep compliance procedures. The EU team also seemed to be undermined by the clashing objectives of its member states, who often freelanced when national interests dictated.

It will sound surprising, and I thought so at the time, that assistance for reform from Myanmar's fellow Association of Southeast Asian Nations (ASEAN) members was limited. Role models though some of these countries were, few had outreach programs of any substance for fellow member states. The one exception was Singapore, which provided useful ideas, and the resources to help achieve them, for civil service reform. The Singapore Embassy was also about the best informed on Myanmar among all the diplomatic posts. This, and the frankness with which they shared their insights, made them disproportionately influential interlocutors.

Japan stood a little aloof from the other development partners, but in a quiet and unobtrusive way provided more hard cash than any other bilateral partner. Japanese representatives would turn up at meetings, make few demands, and contribute little to policy discussions. Their focus was on individual projects, including some very good ones in rural Myanmar, which were invariably completed on time and on budget.

South Korea does not come first to mind as a provider of international aid, but in Myanmar it was a key player. Not least in this context was its pivotal support in the creation of the Myanmar Development Institute (MDI). Modelled on the storied Korea Development Institute (KDI), the MDI was tasked with the development of longer-term policies that would allow Myanmar to follow a path of genuinely transformational growth and development. Staffed with development experts from KDI and other Korean institutions, MDI was also a training vehicle for young Myanmar economists selected for their potential as future policymakers. I had the immense privilege of being the (unpaid) Director of Research at MDI, where I worked alongside my Burmese colleagues in a range of projects. Together, we published the bi-annual *Myanmar Economic Bulletin*, the first such publication in Myanmar fusing cutting-edge economic ideas with applied policy recommendations. The *Bulletin,* which was modelled on the highly influential *Bulletin of Indonesian Economic Studies*, sold out every edition we issued.

Russia, so prominent after the coup in Myanmar when both ruling regimes were bereft of friends, was nowhere to be seen in the early days of the NLD government. Over time, however, its links with Myanmar's military became more visible. It supplied a steady stream of advanced weapons most prominently in the form of fighter aircraft, and provided training and other support to Myanmar's military in cyberwarfare. In terms of our economic reform efforts, Russia was a malign influence throughout.

China was the most secretive and troublesome of all the donor countries in the NLD era. Disdaining all efforts at coordination and often keeping its activities secret from the Myanmar government itself, China's assistance was mostly in the form of self-interested 'megaprojects' that were at least partly about securing for itself key resources, trade routes, strategically located ports, and other geopolitically important assets. Many of these projects were part of the much ballyhooed Belt and Road Initiative (BRI), a global infrastructure development strategy pushed by China more or less everywhere, but aggressively so upon poorer neighbours such as Myanmar.

In contrast to the official development assistance traditionally on offer from donor countries, China's BRI projects came with few if any strings attached in terms of human rights and environmental or social concerns. For many recipient governments, sometimes but not always authoritarian states, this was all part of what made BRI projects appealing. Such attributes had no appeal for Myanmar's reformers.

BRI projects had other problematic characteristics. In a memo I prepared for the State Counsellor in 2018, I made the observations that BRI funding was invariably in the form of loans rather than grants; that these loans were usually at commercial rates of interest; were repayable in 'hard currency', usually US dollars regardless of whether any part of the loan itself was issued in dollars; required some sort of sovereign guarantee irrespective of the actual counterparties; and were usually employed in funding capital-intensive projects that created little in the way of local employment but were highly profitable for Chinese state-owned enterprises. More often than not, these companies turned out to be the instigators of the projects, carefully presented as 'joint ventures' with local entities. Much of the BRI seemed to Myanmar's reformers to be little more than an arrangement by which the Myanmar state would underwrite Chinese state assistance to its own, decidedly enterprising, state conglomerates.

For Myanmar's economic reformers, China was an obstacle and sometimes an opportunity, always to be carefully navigated.

# CHAPTER 2

# Taming dragons:
# Myanmar's banks

'The historical elite capture and misuse of the financial system has made it largely irrelevant to most people in Myanmar . . . Even the most well-intentioned, experienced, skilled policymakers would baulk at the scale of the challenges that lie ahead of them.'

World Bank 2020[22]

In 2016, Myanmar's banks seemed to be on a roll. Shiny new branches were mushrooming across the country, ATMs glowed from street corners, and even internet and mobile-phone banking had entered the promotional lexicon of the country's private banks. The brands and logos of banks crowned the peaks of the rising skylines of Yangon, Mandalay, and other cities. They adorned the shirts of football teams, the sides of buses, and (indicative of the demographics targeted) the airbridges linking a growing fleet of jets landing at Myanmar's airport terminals.

The reality behind the glitter and glamour was otherwise, however, and in 2016 scarcely a bank in Myanmar could have been considered solvent with the application of proper accounting standards. The state-owned banks were largely moribund edifices to sloth and inefficiency while the private banks were little more than corporate cash boxes for crony conglomerates. In all the banks, little in the way of proper credit analysis of borrowers was undertaken, a culture of 'chairman's picks' for lending was endemic, and collateral on loans was routinely overvalued and of uncertain provenance. Settling the payments of corruption and the dispensation of favours was the primary business at hand. The level of non-performing loans in Myanmar's banks was spectacular.

The NLD government was committed to turning this around. A banking crisis was the surest way to bring down Myanmar's economy and stop our reform program dead in its tracks.

Where to start?

We had a roadmap, carefully worked out years before the NLD came into office, that closely approximated the abiding international consensus on banking regulation known as the Basel Accords. In fact, these Accords were already nominally in place in Myanmar via a set of laws largely written by the World Bank and passed by the Thein Sein administration in 2013.[23] But they were Potemkin laws only. No regulations had been written to apply them, and neither the ruling regime nor the manifestly non-independent Central Bank of Myanmar (CBM) had any interest in using them.

Implementing the Basel Accords thus became the reformers' first order of business. To begin with, there was capital adequacy. Capital is basically what a bank is worth, the owners' stake in the business, and what they have to lose should it founder. All other things being equal, the more capital a bank has relative to its assets (the loans and other debt instruments it holds), the safer it is. The Basel requirements set a minimum capital floor that Myanmar's banks, properly accounted for and audited, could not come close to meeting in 2016. But they could get there. They had to get there. And so, that is what the reformers demanded: a sequence of capital thresholds to be met until, finally, the banks would be fully Basel compliant by 2020.

The reader will appreciate the nub of the issue here. Would the owners of Myanmar's banks be willing to stump up the money? To place at risk their own wealth for the good of the whole? They had never been asked before.

Apart from being solvent, a bank also has to have adequate liquidity to make payments as they come due, including to their own customers wanting to draw on their deposits. Such liquid assets can take a number of forms, but they must all be readily convertible into cash without loss or delay. Given Myanmar's long history of financial crises, ensuring that the banks had sufficient liquidity was especially important. There was, after all, nothing quite so panic-inducing as a bank telling its customers it had run out of money.

Being excessively exposed to one borrower, or concentration of borrowers, is also dangerous for a bank. As J Paul Getty is alleged to have put it, 'If you owe the bank $100, that's your problem. If you owe the bank $100 million, that's the bank's problem.'[24] Banking regulators everywhere have imposed limits on large exposures – including in Myanmar. But as per all the other regulations, hitherto these had been observed mostly in the breach. Enforcing these limits, understanding that this would run up against the interests of the banks and their most powerful borrowers, would now be the order of the day.

The banks were greatly annoyed by these new requirements, but of more immediate and indeed existential concern to them was the reformers' next requirement: that banks properly and adequately provision for their non-performing loans. We knew, and they knew that we knew, that this would leave most of them insolvent. And not by a small margin. In the global financial crisis that swept the banking world in 2007–09, non-performing loans of major international banks reached around 7–8 per cent of their portfolios. In Myanmar? Well, we estimated non-performing loans of around 50 per cent for the system and 60–70 per cent for the largest banks. They, and the country, were staring into a financial abyss.

But it was worse, for there was another element spicing it all up. The practice of Myanmar banks, in response to some bad old rules dating from the socialist years, had been to not grant long-term loans but instead simply offer overdraft facilities – rolled over, year after year, sometimes legitimately but too often to disguise credit that would never be repaid. It was all an elaborate game of musical chairs. So long as the music kept playing and Myanmar's central bank and its military overseers kept their eyes and ears closed, all would sail on. Until it couldn't. But that would be another day, a reckoning for later.

For someone else. Meanwhile, the magnitudes grew. Atonement, when it came, would be biblical. Everyone grew to know this, even the banks. To acknowledge it, however, was not done in polite or official company.

Myanmar's reformers had no time for the conventions of the compromised and the crooked. So, in addition to requiring proper accounting and auditing of non-performing loans, we sought to slow the overdraft flow. Banks were told by the Central Bank that:

- For two consecutive weeks, all overdrafts had to be repaid in full.
- Should such overdrafts not be repaid they had to be classified as impaired, and accounted for accordingly.
- Overdrafts that were really long-term loans in disguise had to be converted into term loans with a maximum maturity of three years. Interest payments on these loans had to be made at least quarterly, with reasonable amortisation payments likewise required every quarter.

Then there was the money laundering question.

Seemingly forever, Myanmar had been on the Financial Action Task Force (FATF) 'grey list'. Given Myanmar's role as one of the largest international sources of narcotics (traditionally opium, lately diversifying into methamphetamines), this designation was not unreasonable.

Upon coming into office, Myanmar's reformers' ultimate goal was to get the country off FATF's grey list and allow its banks to be the sort of institutions for which the word 'sanctions' need never again apply. More proximately though, and understanding that FATF's requirements were getting stricter even as its patience grew shorter, we sought to ensure that Myanmar did not slide down onto the 'blacklist', joining the exclusive club that at the time included just Iran and North Korea.

It should have been a straightforward if tough task. Tough it was, but it also proved not at all straightforward. The NLD government was dedicated to eradicating the stain of money laundering. Myanmar's military was not. As already revealed, the military controlled the Ministry of Home Affairs. In turn, Home Affairs had charge of the Financial Intelligence Unit (FIU), the policing body meant to enforce anti-money laundering provisions in conjunction with the Central Bank. And that's where things ran into the sand. Home Affairs did not even allow the FIU to meet with the anti-money laundering team at the Central Bank. On one bizarre occasion in 2017, I attended a contrived 'accidental' meeting between the FIU and the Central Bank in the lobby of a luxury hotel in Naypyitaw to plan some under-the-table progress. It went nowhere, as did other efforts the reformers engaged in. We had the support of international development partners (especially the United Kingdom), but to no avail. In late 2019, we approached the State Counsellor to seek her assistance in moving the FIU from Home Affairs to the Ministry of Planning and Finance. She agreed, but when the military-aligned Vice-President, Myint Swe, brought this issue to the Commander-in-Chief of the armed forces, Senior General Min Aung Hlaing, the military chief blocked the proposal. Post-coup, the efforts of Myanmar's economic reformers to bring an end to money laundering would be used to imprison them. Crime continued to pay in Myanmar.

Related to the money laundering cancer came the question of who should own a bank. 'Fit and proper' persons, said the Basel framework, and so did Myanmar's reformers. In 2019, after much struggle with Home Affairs, the Central Bank issued a series of notifications setting out who could be a director of a bank, run a bank, audit a bank, and be a bank owner.

It was getting personal. And thus came the blow-back to the efforts to fix Myanmar's banks.

At first, the banks were in denial. Non-performing loans, they said, were not a problem. Just look at the annual reports. Nothing to see here. People who said otherwise were troublemakers. Pawns of hidden hands. Foreign hands. Traitors.

Then, for some of the banks, after a time, came an epiphany. Despite all the challenges, Myanmar was a compelling destination for international investors, and there was no better way to benefit from Myanmar's rising prospects than banking. Two, at a stretch three, of Myanmar's banks were investible. Foreign investors, especially from Japan, circled and the funds on offer were tempting. But to access these funds, the banks needed to clean up their act. At a minimum, they would need to comply with domestic banking laws and regulations and, given foreign interest, they needed independently audited proof they were doing so. Deals hovered. And so, fitfully, did progress proceed.

But the recalcitrant banks also evolved, in a way. They got bigger. Their non-performing loans got bigger too, as did the gap between their public financial statements and the numbers in their 'other' accounts. The secret ones. The true ones. Then came 2018, through 2019, into 2020, and the pandemic. A looming election. The recalcitrant banks grew desperate. They started to distrust each other, to withdraw from carefully constructed complex webs of interlocking funding lines. Finally, they turned to the Central Bank, to the state. This was a national problem, they claimed. A disaster loomed. The NLD government had to do something *immediately*. One bank executive, foreign-born and of great experience, sought me out: 'Sean, if we go down, Myanmar's democracy and all of you will go down with us.'

The hitherto complacent but now panicking banks came up with a solution. It was time for the government to create a new bank. A 'bad bank', more formally known as an asset management company, which would buy all the bad debt from the banks and replace it with safe government bonds. Such purchases should be made at par, the troubled banks demanded. They were in no position to absorb any losses. Moreover, the government bonds so swapped must pay them a profitable rate of return. Anything less and a lack of profitability would likewise bring the banks down. Not immediately perhaps, but inexorably. All of them.

This was chutzpah of a very high order. The government was effectively being asked not only to underwrite banks' solvency but their profitability. Myanmar's reformers were not slow in telling the banks this simple truth. Nevertheless, a crisis in the banking sector – it was now late 2020, and the Covid pandemic threatened to shred all the progress that had been made – was the last thing we needed. The reformers enlisted the State Counsellor herself to take some informal meetings with bank owners to impress upon them that the government was not going to allow a banking sector collapse, but nor was it going to bail out the banks in the ways the worst of them wanted. These meetings, we thought, were reasonably successful. Time, however, had just about run out.

At no point during these discussions did we ever consider capital injections from the state. This, readers might recall, was the solution ultimately arrived at by regulators around the world during the global financial crisis of 2007–09. They too had initially gone down the route of trying to take bad assets off the books of the banks (the US Troubled Asset Relief Program, TARP, being the most prominent of these efforts), but had abandoned the plan because pricing bad loans became impossible against a generalised meltdown, and because the scale of the required purchases quickly swamped the available funds. So, regulators just about everywhere simply forced banks to raise capital by taking it from the government. In some cases, this amounted to the nationalisation of banks.

So, why didn't we do the same? I suspect we would have, had the coup not brought our efforts to an end. Our path was not really very different from that facing countries during the 2007–09 GFC; getting a 'just' price for the impaired bank assets would surely have proved a fruitless exercise. Good faith was lacking on the side of the banks, as was the requisite expertise. The second point that must be emphasised is that, given Myanmar's tortured history of state control, we were most reluctant nationalisers. Would that anxiety have been decisive? Probably not. In fact, we were getting the distinct impression that some of the banks were looking at throwing in the towel. The CEO of one of the biggest banks in Myanmar told me in late 2020: 'For a dollar, you guys can have the damned bank.'

At this febrile time I chanced my arm, submitting to the Minister of Finance a proposal to create a government-backed deposit insurance scheme. Such schemes are, in theory, criticised for their promotion of moral hazard (who needs to scrutinise a bank before trusting money to them if your deposits are guaranteed anyway?). But just about every country in the world has them, implicitly if not explicitly. In Myanmar's case, I determined the risk of 'bank runs' as serious and proximate enough to advocate for explicit guarantees. I also judged that, initially, the government would just have to fund such a scheme itself until ultimately a levy on the banks could mean that they and their customers would foot the bill. My proposal, however, was rejected by the Minister, as well as by my reformer colleagues in the Ministry and in the Central Bank. They did not object to my reasoning, but worried that even the *suggestion* that the government would consider ways to protect depositors might escalate fears people had in the banks, and thus cause the very run on deposits we all feared.

*

Banking reform in Myanmar in the years discussed here was about more than just cutting out the rot. It was also about encouraging proper, productive banking. We wanted an expanded sector, not just a stable and law-abiding one.

To this more positive end then, came a number of initiatives, just about all in a liberal, competition-enhancing direction. We removed from the banks the shackles of decades past, manacles to progress that had done little to promote safety even as they malformed credit flows. There was a veritable cacophony of reforms, including removing restrictions on banks against lending on terms of greater than one year, allowing banks to offer home mortgages, expanding the list of property eligible to count as collateral, allowing banks some flexibility on the interest rates they could charge and pay (though we never succeeded to a complete liberalisation on this front), and expanding the ways they could raise capital. The reforms also included allowing foreign banks to take equity positions in Myanmar banks. This would greatly help Myanmar's banks to raise needed capital and could be the vehicle to import new technologies, methodologies, and a renewed sense of what being a bank meant.

In fact, foreign banks had been allowed in Myanmar since 2013. However, characteristic of the Potemkin nature of many of the reforms before the NLD administration, their allowable activities extended little beyond supporting foreign investors and, in practice, usually just those from their home countries. Myanmar's reformers wanted to allow Myanmar to tap into global capital, and trade and exchange linkages more broadly, for which foreign banks were the greatest enablers. Of course, we also had in mind the injection into Myanmar of institutions with deep pockets and the sorts of products that, through the stimulus of competition, might lift the sector more widely. During the NLD government, the activities foreign banks could undertake expanded to more or less the point where there was nothing the local banks did that they could not. Critically, this included lending to Myanmar citizens. Under the NLD, the number of licensed foreign banks in Myanmar increased by nearly 50 per cent, their share of system deposits increased five-fold to just over ten per cent of the total, and their share of total assets tripled.[25]

A final item on the agenda of Myanmar's bank reformers was what to do about the country's state-owned banks (SOBs). There were four major ones, originally created in the 1960s by Myanmar's socialist rulers: one for general business, one for farmers, one for industry, one for foreign trade. All were united in chronically poor management, decrepit facilities, outdated methods, over-staffing, rampant corruption, indifferent (bordering on hostile) service, and levels of non-performing loans that matched those of the private banks. All the SOBs, in short, were decidedly unfit for purpose.

What to do with them? In different circumstances, closing them down and selling off whatever bits of them had value would have been the logical answer. In Myanmar, however, there was a certain nostalgia for some of them, in particular the Myanma Agricultural Development Bank, and some vested interests desirous of keeping things just as they were – a variant perhaps of the idea that, yes, they were SOBs, but they were our SOBs. These interests included SOB staff, whose lowly paid jobs nonetheless offered job security as well as opportunities for equally low-level facilitation payments – 'tea money' in the popular parlance. Naturally, at senior management levels such payments might buy an awful lot of tea.

But there were better reasons for keeping some state presence in banking, which were accepted not just by Myanmar's reformers but even by institutions such as the World Bank. Simply, in Myanmar's highly volatile and fragile banking environment, a safe state-owned 'anchor' institution might not be such a bad thing. The existing SOBs weren't up to this task as constituted, but recapitalised and reinvigorated, they might be. Accepting a $100 million loan from the World Bank to fund it all (only approved by the government after the bank reformers strongly sold the case to the State Counsellor), in 2018 efforts began at merging the Myanma Agricultural Development Bank with the Myanma Economic Bank to create a single institution we hoped would resemble some of the best models around. Our particular focus was the Netherlands' greatly respected Rabobank, whose rural cooperative origins belied its emergence as one of the world's largest, most inclusive and technologically savvy banks. A division of Rabobank was subcontracted to work with the World Bank, and with Myanmar's Ministry of Planning and Finance, to bring it all together. By the time of the coup, progress was well in hand, and choosing the name of the newly merged bank was just one of my agenda items for the State Counsellor's attention in that first week of February 2021.

CHAPTER 3

# Beyond dragons: microfinance, mobiles, and markets

'Banking is necessary, but banks are not.'

Bill Gates, 1994

Banks were at the centre of Myanmar's economy, but they were not the only institutions capable of aggregating and allocating capital. Even in 2016, there was an array of other institutions fulfilling various tasks, some prosaic, others distinctly not. Some were old school, such as the informal *hundi* money transfer business that had been operating throughout Myanmar for a millennia. Others were at the cutting edge, using mobile telephony to create wholly new financial ecosystems.

During the period of the NLD government, the direction of travel was being determined by the new technologies and methodologies introduced by microfinance and mobile money in particular. Meanwhile, at the macroeconomic level, the vision was to develop bond markets to properly finance the state and to create the financial instruments needed to provide for long-term private sector capital formation. All came close to realising their promise.

## MICROFINANCE

Microfinance – banking services for low-income or marginalised groups to promote self-sufficiency – had been operating 'under the radar' of Myanmar's military regime since the early 1990s. By the time the NLD took office in 2016, microfinance was established enough for what we hoped would be rapid expansion with just a little government encouragement and, above all, a loosening of the regulatory leash.[26]

Myanmar's reformers had high hopes for the expansion, but by 2016 some of the global hype around microfinance had subsided. It was no longer seen as a silver bullet for poverty alleviation, but its virtues were real enough in a country such as Myanmar. With the private banks disdainful of poorer customers and, in any case, overwhelmingly concentrated in major cities and towns, microfinance was the best channel to get critical capital into the hands of Myanmar's cultivators and otherwise unbanked micro-businesses. In the traditional telling of the story – largely backed up by experience in Myanmar – microfinance allowed poor households to better protect themselves against fluctuating incomes and financial disruptions. By lending primarily to women, microfinance was said to empower the marginalised and enhance gender equality.[27] The academic research was supportive of the latter, while noting exceptions and complexities. In the Myanmar case, we were convinced about the efficacy of microfinance by what we could see on the ground.

In supporting the spread of microfinance, the NLD government brought in a number of initiatives, most of which were later encoded in a new Microfinance Law (2021) that, while in the parliament and awaiting a final vote, did not survive the coup. Central to the government's thinking was a recognition that microfinance needed to be much more about the provision of safe savings services than about credit. Offering people a debt does not always help them. Another upside to a deposits emphasis was that it automatically brought with it the means by which microfinance institutions in Myanmar could become financially less reliant on (often foreign) donors. That said, we also sought to encourage wholesale funding of microfinanciers by making it easier for them to issue high-denomination bonds and other instruments, including for placement internationally.

The emphasis on deposit taking necessitated improvements in prudential regulation of the sector. Among the regulatory changes brought in by the financial reform team was a host of measures to protect depositors. In one of my last actions before the coup, I had received the go-ahead by Minister of Planning and Finance U Soe Win to develop schemes to ensure the liquidity of microfinance institutions as well as to guarantee their deposits. These were necessary not just in their own right, but also to ensure these institutions were not disadvantaged vis-à-vis the banks following the regulatory changes in that sector.

Other reforms in the new Microfinance Law aimed to free the sector from what we regarded as outdated and unnecessary constraints. Thus the reformers removed the prohibition on microfinance institutions lending on collateral, lifted the cap on the size of their loans (allowing the sector to be more effective suppliers of capital to small, as well as micro, businesses), permitted loan repayment and tenure flexibility (for instance, making loans more useful to farmers by removing the requirement for regular repayments regardless of income, in favour of full repayment at harvest), and brought in new categories of allowable lending such as education loans, emergency loans, family-event loans, and so on. For the first time, Myanmar's microfinanciers would also be allowed to offer microinsurance. To improve consumer protections and guard against excessive indebtedness, mandatory financial literacy programs were introduced along with the establishment of a 'credit bureau' to allow microfinanciers to ensure clients could not take out multiple loans from different institutions.

In Myanmar, the microfinance sector had long been dominated by the Pact Global Microfinance Fund (PGMF), which claimed more than 30 per cent of system lending. Created in the mid-1990s out of a non-government organisation with a special dispensation when microfinance was not legal, it was an especially well-run institution with the potential to become transformative in rural Myanmar. It was stymied, however, by its now obsolete legal structure, which also made it a target for takeover by reform-recalcitrant elements residing in both the military and Myanmar's agriculture ministry. Myanmar's reformers accordingly spent much effort to transform the PGMF into a properly incorporated entity that was investible. At the beginning of 2021, these efforts had borne fruit, and the PGMF was about to announce a transformational investment deal with the renowned microfinance funder, incubator, and innovator Accion International. It was an idea killed by the coup, as ultimately was the PGMF itself.[28]

The success of microfinance in Myanmar during the period of the NLD government was amply revealed in the numbers. By 2020, the sector had six million clients, an increase of 42 per cent in three years. The loan portfolio had swelled across the same period by 385 per cent to K2.2 trillion.[29] This was about ten per cent of total bank lending, meaning that the sector was no trivial player for financial inclusion, especially in rural Myanmar. More than 85 per cent of microfinance clients were women and, before the Covid pandemic hit, the sector was stable. Non-performing loans, at less than one per cent of the loan portfolio, were near non-existent. The future looked bright.

## MOBILES

Well before their time in office arrived in 2016, the reformers in the NLD government drew inspiration from the mobile phone-based transformation of financial services taking place around the world. 'Mobile money', as manifested in the pathbreaking M-Pesa in Kenya and replicas elsewhere, and then via China's giant digital payment firms WeChat

Pay and Alipay, seemed to summon a revolution.[30] Outreach and inclusion appeared to be near complete, limited only by mobile phone possession itself. By 2021, the latter no longer presented a barrier in Myanmar, with the phone-to-population ratio reaching a phenomenal 110 per cent. The Chinese giants even seemed to have located the Holy Grail of lending to small-to-medium enterprises and low-income households by dethroning the tyranny of collateral, substituting it with personal data such that the bane of the banker – what is a borrower's intention? – was supposedly near eliminated.

With mobile penetration high, and an underperforming and unreliable banking system, Myanmar was ripe for a digital transformation. Wave Money, a joint venture between Telenor, the Norwegian telco that had revolutionised Myanmar's mobile phone sector since its entry in 2014, and Yoma Bank, one of the best-run and 'cleanest' of the local banks, was the first and most successful mobile payments firm in Myanmar.[31] Led by an Australian fintech visionary, Brad Jones, at the time the NLD came into government, Wave was already successful, especially as a mobile phone messenger-based cash-in cash-out system using a vast network of more than 50,000 agents by 2020. Most of these agents were themselves small-to-medium enterprises of various shapes and sizes. Later, Wave evolved into true electronic mobile payments (WavePay), in which money was transferred purely digitally via an app containing a mobile wallet, with no necessary recourse to cash at all.

Wave and its quickly following imitators were held back in the years before the NLD government by rules that restricted broader financial services to the banks. Reforms brought in by the NLD opened up the provision of many more financial services by authorised mobile network operators such as Wave. This included offering deposit accounts, and complete freedom in making and receiving payments. To protect depositors, mobile network operators had to meet minimum capital requirements, while at the end of each day the value of the 'float' (total outstanding deposits in the system) had to be deposited into a bank. Further liberalisation measures allowing mobile operators to make loans were at the cusp of implementation when the coup brought the shutters down.

## BOND MARKETS
Building a bond market was something Myanmar's economic reformers took to with alacrity. Such a market was needed to fund the increased government spending to transform health, education,

and all the rest – and to put an end to the money-printing that had been such a scourge. Of course, the reformers were also inspired by the understanding that government bonds were central to the story of nation-building. I fancy there will be enough fans of the musical *Hamilton* among the readers of this book that I need not labour the point. Myanmar's reformers were all devotees.

Myanmar did have something that *looked* like a bond issuing system before the NLD government but, as with so much else, it was all mostly isomorphic mimicry. The Central Bank had sold bonds on behalf of the state, but the purchasers were exclusively the banks – the state-owned ones, the private banks under sufferance, and the Central Bank itself. The whole apparatus was little more than one part of a regime selling financial instruments to another. The bonds were issued at fixed yields, with no open auctions and nothing in the way of a yield curve to properly price Myanmar government debt. It was largely a shell game, with little that warranted the description of a bond 'market'.

In creating a genuine bond market, the NLD government's economic reformers enlisted the support of the Asian Development Bank, as well as the World Bank, the IMF, and the UK's international development arm.[32] From these collaborations emerged a Bond Market Development Master Plan, out of which the government committed to the creation of a local currency debt market in Myanmar that issued a range of government bills and bonds, to be sold in open auctions. Treasury Bills would be short-dated instruments whose sale would aid in the government's liquidity and short-term funding needs. Treasury Bonds, on the other hand, would be offered in maturities of between one and ten years. Bonds and Bills would be sold in competitive open auctions, fully clearing their respective markets and creating a genuine yield curve (a continuous set of prices) from the short to the long term. This, in turn, would be the basis from which *all* debt in Myanmar could be costed, ultimately allowing private sector bond issues and the emergence of a functioning capital market.

A question we faced at this point was whether to seek a sovereign credit rating for Myanmar from the global credit rating agencies (Fitch, Moody's, Standard and Poor's). The obvious answer was surely 'yes'. But we faced a dilemma. Myanmar debt was unrated, so it couldn't be touched by any institution limited to buying investment grade bonds only. This included most banks. On the other hand, unrated bonds were at least not *officially* determined to be junk. Moving ahead to get a designation might just deliver this unhelpful rating. We got advice from the World Bank and some of the bilateral partners, notably the United Kingdom, as well as some pro bono assistance from a couple of the biggest international banks around. In the end, after getting the message that nothing close to an investment grade rating would be forthcoming, we withdrew from the process. Better, we reasoned, to project uncertain risk than certified doubt.

Where would the buyers of Myanmar's government bonds come from? In 2016, the demand side of the market was distinctly under-developed. Up to this time, buyers of Myanmar government debt were largely confined to the Central Bank, eccentric individuals with spare cash and a high risk appetite, and a handful of other banks (often via forced sales). Creating a market for Myanmar bonds required establishing trust as well as the sort of institutions that naturally sought out such investments. Serendipitously, these were at hand in the form of insurance companies, the vibrant emergence of which in Myanmar was a key success of the NLD government. As with other parts of Myanmar's financial ecosystem, prior to 2016 insurance in Myanmar was mostly notable by its absence. There was a largely moribund state institution with a focus on insuring against snake bite, and a few tiny insurance firms owned by some of the banks, but otherwise insurance was a concept barely understood in risk-prone Myanmar. This absence was costly in ways beyond simply a lack of compensation for bad events. In Asia, foreign insurance companies were the largest buyers of government debt. By the nature of their business, insurance companies took on long-term liabilities. They needed to match these with long-term assets. Government bonds fitted the bill nicely.

During the tenure of the NLD government, we opened up Myanmar's insurance market, making it easier to create domestic firms but most importantly, opening up to foreign entities. Vietnam was the model, where foreign insurance companies not only transformed the business of insurance itself but created precisely the investor cohort the country needed to put its public finances in order. From 2016 to 2021, nearly 20 new insurance companies were established in Myanmar, including five fully foreign-owned firms and six foreign-local joint ventures, together including just about all the major global players.[33]

## YANGON STOCK EXCHANGE

Another venue for the sale of bonds presented itself in the form of the Yangon Stock Exchange (YSX).

Created under the Thein Sein government in 2013, the YSX had lived a barely functioning existence for much of its history. When the NLD came to office, just four stocks were listed, trading was sporadic, stock prices were highly volatile and uninformative, while insider trading and other scandals were always just a moment away. With respect to corporate listings, nothing much really changed under the NLD government, but we held great hopes for the usefulness of a secondary board that allowed the listing of firms that did not meet all the criteria of the main board, but which held promise should they be able to raise just a little more capital. And, of course, the YSX would always be a useful venue for the sale of government bonds. Both of these roles were at the cusp of becoming operative as the NLD government prepared for its second term.[34]

## GREEN BONDS

Late in the term of the government, frustrated at the lack of progress in reforming electricity generation in Myanmar (for all sorts of reasons, but including a lack of long-term finance), the economic reform team urged the issuing of so-called 'green bonds'. Very much a market favourite at the time, green bonds were designed to provide long-term financing for renewable energy projects and tap into the substantial funds that development partners and an array of international investors were making available.

To be labelled as truly 'green', such bonds had to meet a number of criteria, including assurances as to their purpose (funding renewables; no fossil fuels), and be subject to external evaluation, reporting, and so on. As a way of stimulating discussion on the idea, I went public in my advocacy in a paper for the ISEAS-Yusof Ishak Institute in Singapore.[35] I suggested green bonds were a necessary instrument if Myanmar was to meet energy investment requirements of around US$2–3 billion per annum across the next decade, much of which would be devoted to solar, which was especially relevant in parts of Myanmar remote from the national grid. To meet assurance criteria and to receive the necessary accreditations, I suggested Myanmar design its green bonds to meet ASEAN's Green Bonds Standards.[36]

This was published on 1 February 2021.

# CHAPTER 4

# Green shoots, setbacks, and escaping China's debt trap

'. . . the atrocities in Rakhine and elsewhere have dramatically elevated the strategic standing of China in Myanmar. For a period following the NLD's ascension, a somewhat chastened China trod warily. Now it is bold and aggressive . . .'

Sean Turnell, in a note to the State Counsellor, 2019

By 2019, the economic reforms instigated by the NLD government had begun to bear fruit – legislatively, institutionally, and in terms of economic performance. Of course, there were problems. Some of these were specifically economic in nature and related largely to the machinery of policy implementation. But the most serious problems were political, including the atrocities committed by Myanmar's military against Rohingya in Rakhine State, and countless abuses in other places. Terrible in themselves, these genocidal campaigns would significantly depreciate the civilian government's political capital to enact economic reform – notwithstanding that such reform offered what few avenues there were to create a better Myanmar. And then there was China, ever looming over Myanmar. It was in dealing with the threat of excessive Chinese influence, and in minimising the debt burdens that came from China's Belt and Road Initiative, that some of the NLD government's biggest successes would come.

## ECONOMIC, LEGISLATIVE, AND REGULATORY REFORMS

Among the sins that critics might levy against the NLD government, that of sloth is the least convincing. In its term of office, the government enacted more than 100 significant legislative, regulatory, and other changes, as well as re-orienting state expenditure. In addition to all the financial liberalisation measures taken up already in these pages, new laws on company formation, investment policy, intellectual property, consumer protections, and tweaks to land laws and bankruptcy procedures aimed to create a business environment conducive to private sector development. In terms of spending, the 2008 Constitution disallowed any control over military expenditure, but allocations elsewhere, especially on health and education, were dramatically increased.[37]

## ECONOMIC OUTCOMES

A singular success of the NLD government's reform efforts was that the country's public finances – the source of that 'original sin' of money-printing and its attending instabilities – had largely been restored along sound and sustainable lines. A timetabled agenda for the reduction of money financing, as agreed with the International Monetary Fund in 2018 to give teeth to the promises in the MSDP, had been achieved ahead of schedule. We were much pleased.

Other metrics were likewise positive. Economic growth was never below five per cent per annum throughout the NLD government's term, inflation was stable, trade and balance of payments deficits were both halved, electricity generation was a little better (on this, more below), tourism numbers were high, and structural change in the economy and greater formalisation of economic life were visible all around.[38] It was not enough for Myanmar's reformers, but we thought it foundational enough to build a bolder second term.

Institution-building was not neglected, with a host of new bodies emerging, not least those designed to lock in better economic policymaking. I have mentioned the Myanmar Development Institute already, but of more immediate impact was the creation of the National Economic Coordination Committee (NECC). The economic reform team had recommended the creation of the NECC in 2017 after witnessing first-hand the in-fighting and turf wars between government ministries. It was meant to act as a clearing-house for policy proposals coming in from different ministries, a forum for review, and a body to determine policy priorities. The NECC was only partially successful, not least because it lacked leadership; the State Counsellor was nominally the Chair, but in practice it was run by a small part-time secretariat. Individual ministries found it fairly easy to make sure their initiatives did not appear before the NECC. In 2019, we sought to give the NECC greater power, including by creating a new position of National Development Coordinator to run it. Analogous to the role of National Security Adviser, the job of the National Development Coordinator was to 'communicate, "trouble shoot", and in other ways steer the government's overall development efforts'.[39] Recognising bureaucracy and 'statism' as obstacles to reform, the Coordinator was to oversee an 'Ease of Doing Business' taskforce charged with slashing red tape and moving Myanmar into the World Bank's top 100 countries for ease of doing business within two years. At the time, Myanmar stood at position 165.[40] To augment their authority, the NDC would be located within the State Counsellor's office. The preferred candidate for the Coordinator role was the aforementioned Deputy Minister of Planning and Finance, U Winston Set Aung. It was all ready to be announced when the coup arrived.

Of similar mixed success were our efforts to reform the Central Bank. On the policy front, success was unambiguous – witness the near ending of money-printing and the commitment to cleaning up the banks. Nevertheless, these successes were really 'extra-institutional', deriving from the extraordinary courage and energy of Deputy Governor U Bo Bo Nge and his links with other reformers such as the Minister of Planning and Finance, U Soe Win, as well as U Winston Set Aung and Min Ye Paing Hein.

Reform of the Central Bank of Myanmar (CBM) itself was less successful. For reasons of political calculation – it was felt we were more likely to get financial sector reform accepted by banks and others if we did not make personnel changes at the top – replacing the Governor of the CBM became a non-starter. This was a pity. Bo Bo and some other reform-minded colleagues within the CBM were able to make a few key appointments at lower levels, and even occasional dismissals, but the bulk of the

CBM's staff remained in place. A job, we impatiently rationalised, for the second term of the NLD government.

## RAKHINE: DISASTER AND DIVISION

The genocidal atrocities committed by Myanmar's military against the Rohingya in Rakhine State brought about the biggest crisis of the NLD government and the greatest challenge to its reform program. There can be no equivocation in condemning the brutality of Myanmar's military in these actions, just as there can be no denying the serious missteps of the civilian government in responding to them. As I have noted already, the civilian government had no control over the military's operations or budget, nor the functioning of the Ministry of Home Affairs or the various militias also involved in the atrocities. Nevertheless, the civilian government should have better communicated its collective repugnance at these actions, the dangers they faced from a military primed to step in at any time (as events would prove), and more effectively reached out to international partners to out-flank the military's hold on Rakhine.

What were we to do?

Frankly, in the personal sense, as well as in the context of the economic reforms, no action could amount to much.

Economics is at the heart of many problems around the world, and economic initiatives can help solve them. Rakhine, and the bestiality of Myanmar's military there, was not one of them. Nevertheless, my privileged access to the civilian government, if not to the military, demanded of me to do something. The horrors perpetrated in Rakhine rocked me to the core and made me reconsider more or less everything I was doing. As I have recalled in my memoir of imprisonment in Myanmar, *An Unlikely Prisoner*, I considered simply leaving.[41] I had come to Myanmar with the purpose of doing all I could to assist in the country's journey to peace and democracy. I had never had any truck with the idea that there was conflict between these objectives and good economics. Indeed, to the contrary. I was not going to hide now behind the noxious idea that a diminution of human rights might be necessary to, as Mussolini had it, 'make the trains run on time'.[42]

So, the first thing I had to do was make sure the State Counsellor, and other civilian leaders, knew fully the international opprobrium building on Myanmar over the military's atrocities. Daw Suu had told me at the start of my appointment that the most important attribute she needed from me was the truth, and that I must never try to second-guess what she wanted to hear about anything. Much blather is now heard about the idea of telling truth to power. To an extent, it has become an almost meaningless cliché for use when nothing is at stake. But it was what I had to do now. It also meant I occasionally had to be an interlocutor between Myanmar's civilian government and friendly governments wanting to vent their anger at what was happening. My truth-telling went both ways, if not always pleasantly for me.

Daw Suu heard me out and thanked me for my honesty. Indeed, she even recalled her instruction to always tell her what I truly thought, but especially the awkward stuff. She told me she was aware of the international reaction to Rakhine, but thought that even close friends under-appreciated her limited room for manoeuvre, the ever-present threat of a coup, and the notion that she might just have ideas herself on how to bring the military to heel. She also expressed her disappointment in former allies, and what she perceived as their fickleness. 'Do they really think I would just abandon the principles over which I was detained for nearly 20 years so easily?'[43]

A second thing I could do was to use the knowledge we had assembled on Myanmar's financial sector, and the way money moved around the country, to gather intelligence on the perpetrators of human rights abuses in Myanmar, and to devise ways they could be brought to justice. Preferably now, but if not, later. The intelligence provided nothing that could stop the atrocities, but it did allow the idea to percolate that there just might be a reckoning at some point. My actions on this front were used against me in my trial after the coup. Following my release from prison in November 2022, however, I was able to share information with international agencies seeking to bring to account those who committed and are still committing crimes against humanity in Myanmar. We shall see.

One final angle I worked on was to join colleagues and some international development partners to try to find economic measures to alleviate the suffering in Rakhine, including among the displaced, and in the longer term create a more inclusive economy. In this, the return of Rohingya to their homes was a precondition. Although we made progress in crafting some viable funding options, in the end this work went nowhere. Anxious that our efforts not be co-opted by the Myanmar military's own plans for Rakhine, we abandoned the endeavour. 'First, do no harm' is a useful injunction for economists, just as it is for physicians.[44]

## SOME OTHER POLICY FAILURES

The civilian government that presided in Myanmar from 2016 made plenty of mistakes. Most governments do, even without the terrible legacy the NLD inherited. It didn't move anywhere near quickly enough to reform the civil service, for instance, notwithstanding the great emphasis the Myanmar Sustainable Development Plan had placed on it. Indeed, it exacerbated the blockages on this front through some ill-considered mergers of government departments that, while looking good in theory, just seemed to suck time and energy. It did little to address ageism in the bureaucracy. By this I don't mean discrimination against older people, as might be more typical in the West. I mean excessive deference to seniority and a bias against the voices of younger people in making changes many of them understood were necessary, but which were too confronting to their 'uncles'.

Of course, to use the word 'uncles' naturally raises the issue of bias against women, which I witnessed daily in Myanmar's civil service. Women sometimes comprised large majorities of staff in ministries such as Planning and Finance. Women occupied many technical and support roles. In my experience, they were invariably better informed than their male colleagues. Yet in meetings they were usually assigned seats at the back. Seldom were they called on to comment. Rarely, very rarely, to lead.

Land reform and the establishment of secure property rights were core objectives of the MSDP, as noted earlier. The reformers even brought to Myanmar the famous international NGO Landesa to kick things off. Around the world, Landesa had helped give practical advice and leadership in all matters relating to land justice.[45] But the task was hard, we ran into many blockages and a certain indifference. Momentum died. Initiating land taxation, a critical component of tax reform and a key revenue source for sub-national governments everywhere, disappeared with it.

One wholly unnecessary policy that distracted the civilian government was the decision in July 2017 to change Myanmar's financial year, which had traditionally run from 1 April to 31 March. The proposal was that this be changed to 1 October to 30 September, to better align Myanmar with international practice, bring the financial year into greater harmony with the country's harvest cycles, and reduce delays in construction projects from a funding-commencement gap caused by the annual monsoon. These were reasonable points, but in my view outweighed by the disruption. The benefits were marginal, and there were more important things to be done.[46] The change was made, but I believe it distracted the government.

Electricity reform, likewise given great attention in the MSDP, was a partial failure. Slowly, policy was turned in the right direction with respect to generating capacity and rehabilitating and expanding the electricity grid, but it was slow going. A poor initial ministerial choice and some bad actors at the top of the ministry meant time went by without anything much changing. Towards the end of the government's first term, we were confident that efforts on renewables would shortly bear fruit and that a November 2019 decision to partially liberalise electricity tariffs would give greater confidence to investors.[47] The coup brought this late progress to an end.

Possibly the most disheartening of all the policy shortfalls of the NLD government was the failure to achieve anything meaningful in decentralising decision-making and administration. Myanmar's states and regions have long been denied any true authority, a situation that only exacerbates ethnic and religious tensions and undermines the substance of democracy. Unfortunately, the NLD government did little to improve matters, and even continued the practice of appointing from the centre the Chief Ministers of most states and regions.

It's hard to imagine that a true and just federal framework that includes an equitable distribution of the country's resource bounty will not be a key part of a better future for Myanmar. Alas, such fiscal federalism was not yet on the table under the civilian government.

## CHINA

One of the most vexing questions facing Myanmar's economic reformers was how to respond to the vaulting ambitions and complicated financing of China's Belt and Road Initiative (BRI), that gargantuan effort to stitch much of the world together through infrastructure, with China at its axis. In Myanmar, the BRI centred mostly on the so-called China-Myanmar Economic Corridor (CMEC) and within this, the Kyaukphyu deep-sea port, special economic zone, and attendant railway and pipelines connecting the port to China's Yunnan Province. Kyaukphyu had all the hallmarks of the BRI-induced debt disasters then becoming apparent throughout the developing world, in particular Sri Lanka's infamous Hambantota Port, a 99-year lease of which had been surrendered to China as collateral on a failed loan.[48]

At an overall cost of US$10 billion, the Kyaukphyu project was much too big for Myanmar's needs, and the debt too large for Myanmar to cope with. As was characteristic, the debt was to be repaid in US dollars, even though not a single dollar would make its way into Myanmar. The project came with no plausible strategy to earn these dollars, elevating foreign exchange risk to the country while imposing great opportunity costs – Myanmar had many better ways to spend scarce dollars. In short, Kyaukphyu unquestionably made strategic sense to China (a port on the Indian Ocean; an alternative to the Malacca Straits!) and brought certain economic benefits too. For Myanmar, it made little sense.

The State Counsellor got the point. The government broadly got the point. A team led by the Minister of Planning and Finance, U Soe Win, the redoubtable U Winston Set Aung, and the equally energetic Deputy Minister of Industry, Min Ye Paing Hein, went to China in late 2018 to renegotiate. The naysayers said it couldn't be done. China was big, rich, and powerful. Myanmar had few options.

But the team returned from China with a new deal for a port to cost just $1.2 billion – a scale to fit any conceivable need Myanmar might have. The railway, and anything else that might be appended to the port, would have to be approved, step by step, only after preceding stages had proved their economic worth. Social and environmental impacts, independently evaluated, would have to be considered throughout. Above all, Kyaukphyu now came with no sovereign guarantee. The Chinese firms promoting the scheme would have to raise funding themselves. No land would be pledged as collateral. A $10 billion debt diplomacy disaster had been turned into a project of modest worth. Nobody was under any illusions; fraught negotiations would doubtless be revisited in the years ahead. But, for the moment, it was an unexpected and astonishing victory.

Naturally, Aung San Suu Kyi was pleased with the outcome and with her reformer team. She told me, however, that this would surely confound the international commentariat who, with little in the way of evidence, had decided she was 'pro-China'. 'I'm not pro-China, nor pro-anyone else but Myanmar.'[49]

Seeking to lock in the principles established in the wake of the Kyaukphyu renegotiations, Myanmar's finance ministry in early 2019 issued a broad statement on future BRI projects.[50] All had to conform to Myanmar's own economic plans and objectives (the MSDP was named in this respect); all projects would have to be subject to open tendering, in theory meaning non-Chinese firms would have a chance to win contracts; all projects had to be open to funding from any source, including the multilateral financial institutions, and not be tied to any particular lender; all would have to conform to environmental, social, and labour safeguards.

Naturally, not every party was happy, China least of all. It had agreed to the Kyaukphyu changes, but privately made clear its displeasure at media reporting that US officials had played a key behind-the-scenes role in the renegotiation. In fact, reports of foreign involvement were greatly exaggerated – the Kyaukphyu negotiations were, in all their important aspects, completely under the charge of Myanmar's reformers. But Beijing's sensitivity on this front was acute. Yun Sun, a prominent China-Myanmar watcher at the Stimson Center in Washington, reported at the time that:

[China] feels particularly betrayed by the fact that the Myanmar government turned to the United States government for technical assistance on the downsizing of the Kyaukphyu deep-sea port. Potential US involvement in the assessment of other CMEC projects is likely to have a negative effect on Chinese interests. For the Chinese, Myanmar is not an easy place to invest due to complicated perceptions of China. To add the involvement of another foreign country with a pre-existing bias towards BRI is unlikely to make it any easier.[51]

Myanmar's military, and entities connected to it that stood to be richly rewarded by BRI contracts, were also aggrieved. This was bluntly communicated to Myanmar's reformers upon their arrival home. Later, the charge of undermining Myanmar's interests in favour of 'hostile powers' was just one of many made against me and my fellow accused following the coup.[52]

Tensions with China over Myanmar's economic reform agenda persisted. Kyaukphyu was the largest of the BRI projects, but other Chinese megaprojects were just as awkward. The Myitsone hydro-electric dam project that had been agreed by Myanmar's then military regime in 2006, suspended since 2011 but persistently pushed by China, would have created a reservoir of 173 square kilometres at the confluence of rivers that formed the Irrawaddy in the country's politically sensitive Kachin State.[53] The dam would generate 6000 MW of electricity, effectively doubling Myanmar's installed electricity generating capacity. But in an extraordinary example of how little Myanmar's military regime understood about the circumstances of the people and economy it ruled over, 90 per cent of this electricity would be exported to China's Yunnan Province.

To be built and operated as a joint venture between China's State Power Investment Corporation

(80 per cent), the Myanmar Ministry of Electric Power (15 per cent), and the Asia World Company (a Myanmar entity with strong China links, five per cent), Myitsone's cost was put at US$3.6 billion. Funding came courtesy of long-term loans from Chinese state-owned banks at commercial interest rates.

Tens of thousands of people were expected to be displaced by the dam (more than 10,000 already by the time of suspension in 2011), with many more livelihoods imperilled downstream. Extra anxiety came from the widely and plausibly held belief that the dam was being built in a region of considerable seismic activity.[54]

In a rare example of responsiveness to public concerns, the newly installed Thein Sein government bowed to popular pressure in 2011 by suspending construction of Myitsone. The then NLD opposition welcomed this, and upon coming to office in 2016 not only continued with the suspension but sought the project's complete cancellation in negotiations with Chinese officials. This time, it did not find a willing negotiating partner, with the consequence that Myitsone continued to be a sore point throughout the NLD government's tenure. A particular irritant was China's routinely dropped hint that cancellation of Myitsone would trigger a compensation payment of US$800 million.[55] All remained unresolved by the time of the coup.[56]

Meanwhile, a very 21st-century vexation in the Myanmar-China relationship emerged courtesy of intrusions by China's aforementioned giant payments firms, Alipay and WeChat Pay, into Myanmar's payments system. Payments systems are the essential plumbing of a country's financial system. Comprising the 'pipes' that connect banks with their customers to enable funds to flow from one counterparty to another, payments systems are fundamentally important but rather dull material. Few glamorous banking careers are fashioned on the basis of expertise in payments.

Since the arrival of digital finance, however, all this has changed, and payments have suddenly become the launchpad from which fintech is challenging hitherto seemingly invulnerable incumbents. We have noted already the rise of Wave Money and its competitors in Myanmar, and the real difference they were making to the lives of so many.

The essence of the problem here was that many Myanmar enterprises (hotels, exporters, importers, and so on) had cross-border accounts with Alipay and WeChat Pay and used them to conduct trade with Chinese firms and nationals. The result was a Chinese currency 'closed loop' carved out of

Myanmar's monetary system, and accordingly without contact with Myanmar's monetary policies, tax net, or data collection systems.

The dangers of this 'renminbisation' of Myanmar's monetary arrangements were recognised by some key reformers in the Central Bank of Myanmar, most notably the ever-energetic Deputy Governor, U Bo Bo Nge, who had launched efforts to create a functioning local payments system and to properly integrate Alipay and WeChat Pay transactions within it. These efforts were being resisted by a number of players in Myanmar, not least the local banks. The announcement of a national payments system that would safeguard against digital 'walled gardens' was to be announced to the new parliament some time in that first week of February 2021.

CHAPTER 5

# The coming of Covid: new plans for a changed world

'The Covid-19 pandemic has delivered a profound shock to our world. Lives have been lost, businesses devastated, hopes and dreams have been set back . . . But the time has now come to extend our efforts to economic recovery as well as relief – and to continue still further on the economic reform journey we began just four years ago.'

Daw Aung San Suu Kyi, January 2021[57]

It's hard to recall now, but as Covid-19 swept the world in the first half of 2020, much considered opinion had it that Southeast Asia would escape the worst of it. With relatively youthful populations already exposed to SARS (severe acute respiratory syndrome) and other semi-seasonal pandemics, the countries of Southeast Asia were thought to enjoy a degree of natural protection. This would prove a delusion.[58]

The threat of Covid was noted early by Myanmar's economic reformers, partially because of their keen focus on events in China but also via their growing aptitude for detecting risk. Real mobilisation, however, began around March 2020, the same month that the World Health Organization declared the coronavirus a global pandemic. By then, the international signs were ominous, and all pointed to the economic storm ahead for Myanmar: collapsing tourism numbers, falling textile and commodity exports as markets closed and shipping contracted, emerging supply constraints on medical and health products together with soaring prices of the same, and declining international remittances as workers overseas were forced home. With all this came pressure on Myanmar's balance of payments and budgetary positions, both of which the economic team estimated would move substantially into deficit. Likewise trending down were our estimates of Myanmar's GDP growth – from a predicted 6.7 per cent for 2020 (second only to Vietnam in the region) to just 0.5 per cent. Uncertainty and anxiety grew.[59]

Myanmar's economic reformers turned their attention away from structural reforms and towards the increasingly urgent need to stimulate the economy. To this end, in April 2020 we came up with the Covid-19 Economic Relief Plan (CERP), devised to alleviate the economic impact of the pandemic as well as to allow for a quick and strong recovery. The CERP included a vast array of measures, but first up was to improve the macroeconomy through monetary easing. Beginning from 1 May 2020, the official interest rate was reduced in stages by a third; banks' required reserves ratios were cut by 30 per cent; credit auctions injected extra liquidity into the banking system; and the exchange rate was allowed to fall according to market supply and demand, which had the effect of boosting the domestic incomes of hard-hit exporters. The government and its reformers even allowed for greater central bank financing of the deficit. We didn't lose our heads – this was a one-off, agreed through gritted teeth. But this was also no time for counterproductive austerity.[60]

To further ease the impact of Covid on the private sector came cuts and payment deferrals on income and commercial taxes as well as customs duties, and the elimination of trade imposts on medical and health products. Electricity tariffs were dramatically reduced, even to zero for the sort of low-level use typically relevant for low-income households.

The electricity tariff reductions would be brought in immediately (1 May 2021), the tax and duty reductions in two stages in June and September 2021.[61]

New and cheap finance was also key to the CERP. Low interest loans to a total of K500 billion (at the time, around US$400 million) were made available through the Myanma Economic Bank to medium and small enterprises, with particular emphasis on the textiles and tourism sectors. A special agricultural loan facility of K600 billion, which became active in August 2020, gave credit to farmers at less than a third of the pre-Covid interest rate. Loan terms and payment schedules were extended. A credit guarantee scheme of up to K300 billion was made available to enterprises ineligible for other types of cheap loans. These were conditional, however, upon firms maintaining employment levels and re-hiring people already laid off.[62]

For people who could sell only their labour, a scheme of unconditional cash transfers was devised. Modest at first, two tranches of payments of K20,000 each, or around US$16, were made to more than 5.5 million households deemed vulnerable or at risk. This scheme was highly innovative both as a method of promoting welfare and because it was delivered by mobile financial service providers. Social security fees for insured workers, mostly in government or large companies, were suspended.

Extra spending on infrastructure was core to the CERP – much of it necessary and useful, but its importance here came more from employment creation. The construction and maintenance of school buildings and rural roads, improvements to irrigation, the installation of simple health facilities such as hand-washing stations – all were included in the CERP, with a cost to the budget of around K500 billion.

Special provision had to be made for the banks, whose unsteady condition we have discussed ad infinitum in these pages. In addition to the liquidity and reserves measures already noted, banks were given a three-year extension of the deadlines to meet their critical prudential ratios, with full compliance now extended to 2023. Given all the drama in trying to get the banks to meet these ratios throughout the tenure of the NLD government, this one hit us reformers hard. Yet it had to be done. Banks were also given greater flexibility in rescheduling and restructuring loans before assigning non-performing loan status. Finally, banks could access a special K100 billion facility to extend cheap trade finance to exporters.

Microfinanciers were hit especially hard by Covid. At the heart of the microfinance model was deep immersion into the localities and lives of members, but this was precisely what Covid precluded. As Myanmar went into increasing lockdown from August 2020, loans in microfinance institutions went bad at unprecedented high single-digit rates. To help them through it, an emergency K55 billion lending facility was set up at the state-owned Myanma Economic Bank.

All up, Myanmar's reformers estimated the CERP would cost just over K2000 billion. How to fund all of this? A ten per cent redirection of budget allocations across all other areas of government was a first internal step. The successful efforts to create a bond market were likewise promising. Less pleasing to contemplate was the recourse to central bank funding, but it was there, at least for the short term. In a joint letter to the International Monetary Fund in June 2020, Myanmar's Minister of Planning and Finance and the Governor of the Central Bank of Myanmar sought to assure that none of this Covid relief signified a change of long-term policy, and that they aimed to 'guard against the risks of excessive monetization' by limiting central bank financing 'to about 5 percent of reserve money . . . consistent with broader monetary targets for the next two fiscal years and to phase out monetary financing thereafter as the economy begins to recover.'[63]

Most pressing was the need for international finance. The balance of payments was becoming increasingly precarious, while debt payments were due. But by now, the international financial community was belatedly mobilising. Myanmar had a number of options, the first of which was the Debt Service Suspension Initiative supported by the G20 and Paris Club of creditor nations, from which Myanmar received around US$300 million. Independent of this support came around US$200 million of assistance from Japan, as well as all manner of in-kind support from the United States, the United Kingdom, South Korea, and Australia, mainly in the form of medical equipment. The one country that offered Myanmar little real assistance was China, notwithstanding its position as by far Myanmar's largest creditor, its extravagant claims of fulfilling a protective role to a country it so often portrayed as a 'little brother' (commonly rendered as *pauk-phaw* in Burmese), and the pressure it continued to exert for approval of various Belt and Road Initiative projects.

Of course, the multilateral financial institutions were key targets for funds, and Myanmar received early concessional loans from the World Bank and the Asian Development Bank of around K300 billion each. Much of this was re-purposed credit originally granted for longer-term projects. It was a pity to lose this. The need, however, was now.

The IMF has a reputation, partially deserved, for being parsimonious when generosity is called for. This time, however, it rose to the occasion. Allowing countries to access emergency financing under its Rapid Credit Facility/Rapid Financing Instrument, Myanmar was able to request an immediate draw-down of US$357 million. This was 50 per cent of the country's 'quota' of routinely available funds via the IMF. The remaining 50 per cent was also available, for later.[64]

So far, so good. Through 2020 and into 2021, all of these emergency measures staved off both the rapid spread of Covid and the collapse of the economy. There was great suffering, and the country went into substantial lockdown in September 2020. Nevertheless, Myanmar's economic team thought it had dodged catastrophe. Maybe the worst was over. We even started to think again about the long term. How and when to begin to remove all the potentially inflation-provoking short-term stimuli and get back on the reform track?

Accordingly, as 2020 drew to a close, a new post-Covid reform re-boot, the Myanmar Economic Resilience and Reform Plan (MERRP), was drawn up.[65] Grabbing the opportunity to push for bigger reforms, incorporating lessons from the past, and in the knowledge that the NLD's November 2020 election win (in which it took 83 per cent of the seats contested) had created new political capital for being bolder and better, the MERRP would be the manifesto the reformers always wanted.[66] Social and environmental considerations were prominent, alongside the hard tack of greater monetary liberalisation – mandated interest rate caps and floors would finally go, allowing credit to be priced for risk. The MERRP would also allow for the introduction of a uniform 'revenue tariff', bringing coherence to import policy while also creating a foundation upon which a broader VAT could be crafted; the establishment of a 'proper' asset management company to deal with bad bank debt; the creation of a 'Project Bank' to bring transparency and true cost/benefit accounting in infrastructure procurement; and a program through which banks could 'rediscount' loans to exporters at the Central Bank of Myanmar, putting more flesh on the bones of an export-led growth strategy. There were a myriad of other items, but the above alone gave us hope that the path ahead might be clearer than the one traversed.

The final draft of the MERRP was completed on the last day of January 2021. I was asked to bring a hard copy to Myanmar's capital, Naypyitaw, for final review and approval by the State Counsellor and her ministers. A meeting was set for Thursday, 4 February 2021.

# CHAPTER 6

# Coup: Myanmar's great economic leap backwards

'They make a desert and call it peace.'

Tacitus, *The Life of Agricola*, AD 98

On 1 February 2021, the Commander-in-Chief of Myanmar's military, Senior General Min Aung Hlaing, took power in a coup against the civilian NLD government. Complaining of anomalies in the elections of November 2020, Min Aung Hlaing and his newly assembled junta immediately arrested Daw Aung San Suu Kyi, most of her ministers, as well as officials across the civilian government. In the following days the net widened, ensnaring all the reformers hailed in these pages. On 6 February, this included me. By now, the country was in revolt against a junta that prosaically styled itself the State Administration Council. Killing opponents was soon added to the practice of jailing them, and Myanmar descended once more into military dictatorship.

Dismembering and reversing the economic reforms that had played out in Myanmar since 2010, but especially under the civilian NLD government, was a central objective of the new junta. It needed financial and other resources to suppress the growing rebellion. Purloining resources to military ends is a characteristic of such regimes anywhere, but in the Myanmar context, and in light of the junta's particular savagery following the coup, this objective was existential. The new regime was outnumbered on the ground and needed air power and advanced weaponry to survive. This required foreign exchange. Real money. Money they couldn't simply print.

The junta's other economic motivation was a mix of the loosely ideological and the nakedly self-interested. Min Aung Hlaing and his team had long been hostile to the liberalising approach of the NLD government, preferring state direction to decentralised economic freedom and the outcomes of the market.

However motivated, the anti-reform agenda of the junta didn't take long to express itself in policy reversals. Within a few months, it had dismantled the NLD government's Covid relief measures and largely ignored the Covid-19 Economic Relief Plan and the Myanmar Economic Resilience and Reform Plan. Together with the chaos and conflict generated by the coup, Covid infection rates soared and Myanmar became one of the most Covid-impacted countries in the world. All was exacerbated by the junta's arrests of nurses, doctors, and other health professionals.[67]

The State Administration Council also returned Myanmar to a fixed exchange rate regime, accompanied by ever-tightening exchange controls. These effectively expropriated the foreign exchange earnings of overseas Myanmar workers by forcing the conversion of remittances into the fast-depreciating *kyat* (more on this below). New taxes on overseas corporate and individual earnings, and prohibitions on foreign currency bank accounts, completed the autarkic currency zone to which Myanmar citizens were now confined.

Car imports were banned, a range of consumer items were deemed 'luxuries', and import restrictions were imposed on fuel and cooking oil.[68] The system of import licensing, largely disbanded in the liberalisation policies of the NLD, was imposed on more than 75 per cent of import items.

Myanmar businesses with foreign debts were urged to suspend repayments of both principal and interest.[69] This extraordinary directive, which came from the now junta-controlled Central Bank of Myanmar, made debt default a sovereign policy, shredding Myanmar's fragile credit-worthiness in the process.

By the end of 2023, state spending on health and education was 15 per cent below that of 2019, while spending on the military was up 63 per cent across the same period.[70] Long one of the few countries in which health and education spending *combined* was less than that allocated to the military, by 2023 spending on the latter was almost twice that of the former.

The SAC abrogated all commitments to fiscal prudence and sound public finance. The bond market and taxation initiatives of the NLD were abandoned, with 'printing money' accounting for more than 70 per cent of the 'financing' of Myanmar's growing budget deficits.

The junta introduced price controls and rationing measures on an array of food and other products in a misguided attempt to control inflation. Shortages and the strengthening of the underground economy were the inevitable outcomes.

Myanmar foreign policy was realigned to side with those few countries willing to recognise the State Administration Council as the legitimate government, including Russia and China. The former was a supplier of little more than arms, which it would only supply to Myanmar in exchange for non-US dollar hard currency, or gold. The China shift inevitably put back on the table many of the giant infrastructure projects proposed as part of the Belt and Road Initiative, the debt risks from which had been carefully avoided by the NLD government. The junta threw out hints it was willing to reconsider any or all of these projects, including Kyaukphyu and Myitsone. Growing doubts in China over the junta's ability to provide the necessary security has meant not much has happened on this front. Yet.

For a while, the State Administration Council also denied bank customers access to their deposit accounts. Such restrictions – applied on and off throughout the early months of the junta's rule – were designed to curtail 'bank runs'. But nothing could be more destructive of trust, the one truly indispensable asset financial institutions must have.

In February 2024, the junta reintroduced compulsory conscription for all males aged 18 to 35 and all females from 18 to 27. Doctors and unspecified other professionals can be drafted up to the age of 45. Service is supposedly two years. This ultimate loss of property rights (to one's own person) is already being strongly resisted, and is regarded by most observers of Myanmar as a spectacular 'own goal' by an increasingly desperate regime.[71]

All these measures, many of which were eagerly reported to Myanmar's reformers in our respective prisons, had severe repercussions for the economy. Any notion that the country was in some type of reformist 'transition' disappeared. Myanmar was not going along any sort of trajectory except down, with the imagined endpoint of policymakers little more than regime survival.

The numbers were unforgiving: GDP down 18 per cent across the year following the coup, and at the time of writing (mid-2024), it remains ten per cent below pre-Covid levels. Myanmar is the only country in Southeast Asia not to have recovered to pre-Covid output. The proportion of Myanmar's population below the poverty line now stands at 40 per cent, double the proportion before the military takeover. Inflation accelerated post-coup as goods came to be in short supply and production chains were disrupted by fighting. In 2023, inflation in Myanmar was, at 29 per cent, more than six times the average of the other ASEAN member states. A representative 'common diet' food basket cost 140 per cent more in Myanmar in 2023 than it did in 2019.[72]

Myanmar's *kyat*, never a strong store of value, went into freefall after the coup. In August 2022, it hit a low of more than K4000 to US$1, and in mid-2024 was once again testing these depths.[73] Falling exports, a collapse in foreign direct investment, and severe capital flight all combined to undermine the local currency. The low value of the *kyat* might have, in more normal circumstances, stimulated tourism as Myanmar became a dramatically cheaper destination for holidaymakers. Alas, conflict and chaos determined otherwise, and in 2023 the number of tourists to Myanmar remained just a third of those arriving in 2019. Such tourists are largely short-stay small spenders from China and other neighbouring countries. Myanmar as a bucket-list destination for high-spending tourists from Europe, North America, and Australasia has become a thing of the past.

The supply of electricity – insufficient before the coup, as discussed – was down ten per cent at the end of 2023 compared to 2019. Blackouts, common enough before, have become routine. Energy costs to manufacturers, more reliant than ever on diesel generators and their increasingly expensive fuel, erode any theoretical comparative advantages in labour and other costs. Sanctions and reputational issues that have led to the withdrawal of many international clothing brands have stopped the growth of Myanmar's garment sector.[74]

With military spending unleashed and taxation revenues in disarray as the formal economy shrinks, Myanmar's public debt has sharply increased. Even as money-printing bore some of the burden (but brought with it inflation in the time-proven manner), Myanmar's state debt went from a comfortable 42 per cent of GDP in 2020 to 63 per cent in 2023. Foreign debt increased in *kyat* terms as the currency declined in value, even as new international financing was closed off. Bilateral and multilateral development partners have largely suspended their interactions with Myanmar.[75]

Falling foreign investment, noted above in the context of financial flows that might have supported the value of the *kyat*, has even more serious long-term implications. Prominent here is the cessation of exploration for potential new offshore natural gas fields. Existing fields have been both a primary source of Myanmar's energy supplies as well as a key source of foreign earnings through exports, mainly to Thailand and China. In the absence of investment to seek out new fields and the accelerating exhaustion of existing ones, Myanmar's energy exporting future looks bleak.[76]

Myanmar's banks, on the brink throughout the NLD era, now limp on as little more than zombie entities held upright only by the understanding that the ruling junta will not permit their collapse. None of the underlying problems have been fixed, indeed with incomes down and debts up, the non-performing loan situation in Myanmar's banks can only have grown considerably worse.

Microfinance, that sector of hope and expectation during the NLD and earlier years, has suffered greatly in the wake of the coup. Coming on the back of disruptions under Covid, regime pronouncements suggesting that clients not repay past loans undermined micro-lender balance sheets still further.[77] In 2024, microfinance loans 'at risk' amounted to more than 30 per cent of the total portfolio of the sector, an astonishing proportion given that the same ratio was less than one per cent in 2019. The junta's ban on Myanmar entities repaying foreign creditors likewise did great damage. As we have seen, in Myanmar the major microfinanciers were just about all foreign funded. The State Administration Council's actions severed the sector's vital capital source in the short term and undermined its credibility in the longer run. As a result, microfinance has contracted in Myanmar, with 300,000 fewer clients in 2024 than in early 2021. While there have been signs of stabilisation more recently, demand for micro-credit now vastly exceeds supply.[78]

Myanmar's microfinance sector has also been roiled by the clumsy efforts of the regime to expropriate the country's largest microfinance institution, the Pact Global Microfinance Fund (PGMF). Long a target of the avarice of people connected to Myanmar's military and accounting for more than 30 per cent of the entire sector's assets, the coup was a disaster for the PGMF.[79] It was quickly prohibited from making any new loans, its foreign staff denied visas, its local staff harassed. The junta sought to direct credit to individuals and entities aligned to it, and upon meeting principled resistance from the PGMF, cancelled its operating licence. Seeing no future in Myanmar, in June 2023 the PGMF's foreign owners declared 'game over'. Forgiving US$156 million in outstanding loans to nearly 900,000 borrowers, the microfinance institution closed its operations.[80] More than one million clients lost access to financial products and services.

Also limping on post-coup was mobile financial services. In a terrible inversion of its promise, this technology, which should have been about expanding inclusion and financial freedom, became a tool via which the junta monitored and punished its opponents.[81] The mobile phone as liberator became the mobile phone as enslaver. Market leader in the industry, Wave Money, was disrupted by the departure from Myanmar of Telenor, its Norwegian founding owner and provider of its mobile platform.[82] Wave Money's closest competitor, KBZPay, also suffered from the regime's scrutiny of its customers.[83] By mid-2024, the industry had stabilised somewhat and was providing useful (non-politically sensitive) payment services, but the excitement and hope had evaporated.[84]

## *HUNDI*'S RESSURECTION

In place of emergent formal financial services and high technology has come the resurrection of Myanmar's *hundi* system of informal written orders directing that a person must pay a certain sum of money to another named in the order. This ancient instrument of transferring monetary value under the noses of authority has a long history in Myanmar.[85] Mobile phones and digital money had increasingly marginalised it during the NLD years. Its reliance on personal trust and informal processes seemed to have no place in a fast-modernising economy based on law and formal procedures. So it might have continued, but the need for the people of Myanmar to once again escape the depredations of their rulers has brought *hundi* roaring back. The regime has tried to suppress it, reverting once more to the time-honoured practice of arresting *hundi* dealers, but to no avail. In Myanmar, *hundi*, as well as physical cash, continues to constitute 'coined liberty'.[86]

## SANCTIONS RETURN

The efforts of Myanmar's economic reformers to create what we liked to call the 'last and best' of Southeast Asia's high-growth economies were blown away by the country's return to the world's ostracised squad. Reacting to the brutality and wanton destruction of the regime, and reflecting the near-global revulsion at what was taking place, Western countries hurried to re-impose sanctions. The United States was the leader, but it was quickly followed by the United Kingdom, the European Union, Canada, Australia, much of Scandinavia, and sundry others. The measures included targeted financial sanctions on individuals as well as military-linked enterprises and banks, and visa and travel bans on regime officials. Reflecting the regime's ruthless use of air power against its own people, bans on the export of jet fuel to Myanmar have become an increasing focus.[87]

Myanmar's return to pariah status has been accelerated by its designation on the Financial Action Task Force's money laundering and terrorist financing 'blacklist', the outcome Myanmar's reformers had worked so hard to avoid throughout the NLD government years. Of course, the move was entirely justified. The commitments and progress made under the NLD have been negligently rendered void by the junta, which, as we shall see shortly, openly positioned Myanmar as a jurisdiction in which crime – including international financial crime – could flourish.

In 2024, Myanmar was expelled from the Extractive Industries Transparency Initiative (EITI). Acknowledging the great progress Myanmar had made in recent years in improving governance in the extractive sector (mostly the result of the efforts of some truly splendid local non-governmental organisations), the EITI said post-coup instability and conflict 'made it unfeasible to uphold key aspects' of the Initiative.[88] The EITI also noted that the regime had, in any case, effectively dissolved a stakeholder group comprising non-government actors, meaning that 'no independently verified information' had been published on the extractive sector in the 'last three years'. Intimidation, repression, and the curtailment of free speech were once again characteristics of the country, as was an egregious 'deterioration in space for civil society'. Perhaps wanting to give some hope, the EITI governing board declared that 'if conditions improve', Myanmar still had 'the opportunity to reapply for EITI membership'.

*

Accompanying the transformation of Myanmar's economy has been the corresponding shift in the country's management. Gone are the elected MPs and much of the technocracy, reformist and otherwise. In their place have come the generals at the top and a rash of colonels who proliferate throughout what was once Myanmar's policymaking bodies. Armed with the confidence that follows the cowering of defenceless civilians before them, the decisions of these men in khaki are as assured as they are usually wrong-headed. To the khaki clan, however, economics is less about incentives, sentiment, secure property rights, sound money, and other similar wishy-washy notions than it is about simple logistics. If you want a new industry, order its creation! Compel compliance. Sure, some people will be ungrateful. Resistant even. But, well, that's the price that comes with being a steward of people who know not what is best for them. Or something like that.

What has happened to the old economic decision-makers? In the private sector, many initially joined the resistance (bank employees seem to have been unusually prominent early protestors against the coup) before settling back into sullen survivalist acquiescence. In the public sector, mass resignations, sackings, and imprisonments have left a cadaver that the aforementioned colonels lord over. Disdained by Myanmar's erstwhile development partners, these martial mavens have little contact with and even less knowledge of the outside world. Institutions and bodies such as the National Economic Coordination Committee and the Myanmar Development Institute are gone, their staff scattered. The *Myanmar Economic Bulletin* is no more. At the Central Bank of Myanmar, a new governor reigns, while the policy heads within are military men.

Of the reformers featured in this book, some remain in prison or other forms of detention, some have fled abroad, others are lying low. For some time after the coup, however, we were mostly together, incarcerated first in Yangon's infamous Insein Prison and later in the main jail of Myanmar's capital Naypyitaw. Drawn together thus, we spent a considerable time thinking, talking, and ruminating about the economic reforms discussed in this book. What had gone right, what had gone wrong. Perhaps such circumstances only reinforce the convictions one has been convicted for, but the consensus was unequivocal: we would do it all again, only faster and deeper. Spend political capital when we had it most to remove the obstacles to progress that will always coalesce, given the chance.

None of this surprised me. What did surprise me, in this unusually frank environment, was the testimony of my fellow prisoners about the extent of resistance to our work from Myanmar's security services. I had been aware of aspects of this, but for my Myanmar colleagues, threats from the military and their supporting cohorts were a more routine part of their lives than I had appreciated. All thought Myanmar's banks were complicit in the coup and in financially facilitating many of the subsequent actions of the junta.

Among those who continue to languish in prison is the former Deputy Governor of the Central Bank of Myanmar, U Bo Bo Nge, sentenced to 20 years for having the temerity to try to protect Myanmar's international reserves from depredation and corruption. Of course, this group also includes Daw Aung San Suu Kyi. Convicted alongside myself for supposed breaches of Myanmar's Official Secrets Act, in essence she was accused of being my agent, with me as spy and handler. Today, she still resides in prison in Naypyitaw, in uncomfortable conditions and uncertain health. In my last conversation with her in November 2022, she expressed her pride in the people of Myanmar, but especially the young, in standing up against tyranny and injustice.

*

Side-by-side with the descent of the everyday economy has been the growth of Myanmar as a production centre and safe haven for international crime. Under the junta, Myanmar has re-emerged as the world's largest producer of opium, a title wrested from its long-term rival in the business, Afghanistan. In announcing this changeover in the league tables, the United Nations Office on Drugs and Crime unequivocally assigned causation to the 'economic, security and governance disruptions that followed the military takeover of February 2021'.[89]

Other illicit activities have emerged under the junta, the most internationally noteworthy of which has been the mushrooming of criminal enclaves mostly clustered along Myanmar's borders with China and Thailand, hosting gambling and cyber-scam syndicates. Workers in these enclaves are often victims of fraud and trafficking, and little more than forced labour. Meanwhile, the targets of their work are invariably not citizens of Myanmar but Chinese, Americans, and anyone else of means who can be fleeced electronically. The US government-affiliated

Institute of Peace estimates that such targets have lost tens of billions of dollars to scams originating in Myanmar, and that the activities represent a threat to regional and even global security.[90] Implicitly confirming this, and its unhappiness at the junta for allowing the targeting of Chinese citizens for cybercrime, has been China's efforts to issue arrest warrants for junta officials linked to the scams. Even more dramatically, China has supported ethnic armies in Myanmar participating in Operation 1027, a joint military operation conducted by the Three Brotherhood Alliance against the regime.[91]

*

A dispiriting thing it would be to end this book on the growing khaki-isation of Myanmar's economy and its rapid criminal diversification. Equally dispiriting would be to conclude with some uplifting but transparently false bromide as to the country's potential if only the men in green would return to their barracks. Whistling in the dark has its uses, but in Myanmar's case we are rather beyond that.

Luckily, I need not do either of these things. The situation in Myanmar is dire, but it is not without genuine hope. During the writing of this book, the regime has suffered significant reverses on the battlefield and, as at mid-2024, appears more vulnerable than at any time in its dismal tenure. The democratic opposition, constituting the National Unity Government at its core but also the constellation of ethnic armies and others around it, has seldom appeared more unified. Divisions and differences remain, as they do among all peoples seeking freedom, but they have not diminished the revulsion that the junta has a singular ability to inspire.

On the economic front, opposition to the regime combines stalwart defiance with extraordinary creativity. The economic and financial policy teams in and around the National Unity Government need no introduction to the sorts of reforms detailed in these pages. They have added innovative ways of using fintech and bond issues, lotteries, and cheeky auctions of junta leaders' homes to fund the fight and help Myanmar's suffering civilians.[92] Alternative ministries, a central bank, and other institutions develop policies for rapid application when the time comes. All of it is driven and staffed by people who clearly did not waste time in Myanmar's brief window of exposure to better possibilities. With reason, they call what they are doing a Spring Revolution.

Václav Havel, a friend and ally of Aung San Suu Kyi's in the darkest of times, once said that hope was not the conviction that things would turn out well but the 'certainty that something has meaning regardless of how it turns out'. In Myanmar, many things are lacking these days. Hope, defined thus, is not one of them.

# Acknowledgements

Thanking people who have helped you along the way is a rare pleasure available to an author. In the case of Myanmar, however, it can be an extra avenue of torment. The reason is as simple as it is tragic. People in Myanmar, but especially those engaged in the reform efforts of the sort recorded in these pages, remain in great peril. Some are in prison, some are still in hiding, some have taken up arms, some have fled Myanmar but are in precarious circumstances even beyond its borders. What to do? Perhaps the best thing, the fairest thing, especially for someone like me who owes so much to so many people vulnerable in the ways outlined, is to say a collective thank you to Myanmar's reformers, without singling out any in particular. Of course, they know who they are and, at the risk of getting all

Rumsfeldian, they know that I know who they are. Myanmar colleagues, friends – my love, gratitude, respect, is profound and true.

Some people who I *can* thank openly are the wonderful researchers and staff at the Lowy Institute. Fresh from the horrors of my imprisonment and ill treatment, they took a punt on me. Their generosity, their intellectual joie de vivre, their independence and originality shine like beacons. Australia does not have many think tanks, and nothing so well and so justifiably renowned internationally as the Lowy Institute. Thank you especially to the Institute's Executive Director Michael Fullilove, Head of Research Hervé Lemahieu, Research Editor Clare Caldwell, and editor of the Lowy Institute Papers Sam Roggeveen.

To Macquarie University, my alma mater and where I remain an Honorary Professor, thank you for your constant and unwavering support.

Finally, thank you to my partner in all that I do. My Hanoi True Blue, my Ha Vu.

# Endnotes

1   My odd title was invented by Daw Aung San Suu Kyi, and chosen to describe my rather anomalous position as being neither inside nor outside her government. Throughout my tenure in Myanmar, I was never an employee of, and never paid by, its government. Rather, I was subcontracted by Australia's Department of Foreign Affairs and Trade to provide advice to the Myanmar government. I was not a formal employee of DFAT either, which means I ought to say here what is probably obvious – that the views expressed in this book do not reflect the opinions of DFAT, the Australian government, the Lowy Institute, nor anyone else apart from myself.

2   The Washington Consensus was the label coined in 1989 by economist John Williamson to describe the list of policies that helped parts of Latin America recover from chronic macroeconomic crises in the 1970s and 80s. His list, which was meant simply to be descriptive, included such policies as disciplined and well-directed government spending, market-determined interest and exchange rates, reasonable levels of taxation, a welcoming environment to foreign investment, limited state ownership of business,

low barriers of entry to enterprise, and secure property rights. The term is used alternatively to praise or abuse, according to taste and predilection.

3     Albert Hirschman quoted in Michele Alacevich, 'In Praise of Possibility', *Aeon,* 3 August 2021, https://aeon.co/essays/from-probable-to-possible-the-ideas-of-albert-o-hirschman.

4     Louis Walinsky (1908–2001) was Economic Adviser to the then newly independent Burma's first Prime Minister, U Nu. Initially appointed via a US aid program, Walinsky was resident in Myanmar from 1952 to 1958. His work in Myanmar came to an end upon what was, in essence, first a 'soft' military takeover of the country in 1958, followed by the creation of a complete military-socialist state in 1962. From that moment and for the next 50 years, foreign advisers of the likes of Walinsky were decidedly unwelcome in Myanmar. Though there were differences aplenty, my own role in Myanmar from 2016 to 2021 was analogous to Walinsky's as, indeed, were the circumstances of our professional termination. This quote is from Louis Walinsky, *Economic Development in Burma, 1951–60,* (New York: Twentieth Century Fund, 1962).

5     Sean Turnell, *Fiery Dragons: Banks, Moneylenders and Microfinance in Myanmar,* (Copenhagen: NIAS Press, 2009). The name change – Burma to Myanmar – was a decision made by the country's then ruling military regime in 1989.

6     For a brief but comprehensive history of Myanmar that covers most of the events discussed here, see Michael W Charney, *A History of Modern Burma,* (Cambridge: Cambridge University Press, 2009).

7     A half-Burmese, half-English phrase that refers to coating an object in liquid gold to give the impression that it is actually made from the precious metal.

8   For a more positive take on the Thein Sein administration, see Marie Lall, *Understanding Reform in Myanmar: People and Society in the Wake of Military Rule*, (London: Hurst Publishers, 2016).

9   'The Myanmar Elections: Results and Implications', International Crisis Group, 9 December 2015, https://www.crisisgroup.org/asia/south-east-asia/myanmar/myanmar-elections-results-and-implications.

10  Constitution of the Republic of the Union of Myanmar 2008, https://www.constituteproject.org/constitution/Myanmar_2008.

11  Notwithstanding the efforts of Myanmar's current military rulers to expunge it, the MSDP remains accessible on the web. See, for instance, https://themimu.info/sites/themimu.info/files/documents/Core_Doc_Myanmar_Sustainable_Development_Plan_2018_-_2030_Aug2018.pdf.

12  See especially, William Easterly, *The Tyranny of Experts: Economists, Dictators, and the Forgotten Rights of the Poor*, (New York: Basic Books, 2014); Daron Acemoglu and James A Robinson, *Why Nations Fail: The Origins of Power, Prosperity, and Poverty*, (New York: Crown Publishers, 2012). Another influential book among the reformers was Joe Studwell, *How Asia Works: Success and Failure in the World's Most Dynamic Region*, (New York: Grove Books, 2013).

13  And was inspired by the writings of the great Burmese economist Ronald Findlay and his work on the economics of 'Leviathan' (in the Hobbesian sense). Ronald Findlay, *The Political Economy of Leviathan*, (Stockholm: Institute for International Economic Studies, 1984).

14  Myanmar had three approved special economic zones at the time – at Thilawa on the Yangon River, at Dawei in Myanmar's Tanintharyi Region, and at Kyaukphyu on

the Bay of Bengal. They were the creation of legislation introduced by the Thein Sein administration in 2013.

15   For a contemporary overview of the challenge we faced on the electricity front, see 'Transforming Myanmar's Energy Sector', International Growth Centre, 4 October 2016, https://www.theigc.org/blogs/transforming-myanmars-energy-sector.

16   Details of what constituted this basic health package can be found in the NLD government's 'Myanmar National Health Plan (2017–2021)', still available online at https://mohs.gov.mm/Main/content/page/myanmar-national-health-plan-2017-2021-summary.

17   For background, and the story of the partial redemption of this promise made in the MSDP, see *Myanmar Mining Guide*, Dentons Rodyck, 26 March 2019, https://dentons.rodyk.com/en/insights/alerts/2019/march/29/-/media/f7bbf133af8347359cb990a400dad43a.ashx.

18   The speaker was Gevorg Sargsyan, 'Myanmar Intensifies Economic Policy Reform Agenda to Address Emerging Risks and Achieve Inclusive, Sustained Growth', 12 July 2018, The World Bank, https://www.worldbank.org/en/news/press-release/2018/07/12/myanmar-intensifies-economic-policy-reform-agenda-to-address-emerging-risks-and-achieve-inclusive-sustained-growth.

19   Naing Ko Ko, 'The Emergence of Suukyinomics', *East Asia Forum,* 1 March 2019, https://eastasiaforum.org/2019/03/01/the-emergence-of-suukyinomics/.

20   One of these firms was Nathan Associates, the very same company that wrote independent Myanmar's first set of economic plans in 1953: *Economic and Engineering Development of Burma,* (Rangoon: Knappen Tippetts Abbett McCarthy in association with Pierce Management and Robert R Nathan Associates, 1953). Louis Walinsky, discussed above, was the Chief Economist at Nathan Associates in this period. During the time of the NLD

government, Nathan's operations in Myanmar were led by the redoubtable Steve Parker and Lynn Salinger.

21 Led by the head of the economics team at Australia's Yangon Embassy, Tim Vistarini.

22 This, from a document that never saw the light of day following the military coup. Parts of it were later incorporated in *Myanmar Financial Sector Reforms*, World Bank, 8 July 2022, https://documents1.worldbank.org/curated/en/099950007082234868/pdf/P17700209b1e6603e0822b0be869cb8882b.pdf.

23 Notably the *Central Bank of Myanmar Law* of that year.

24 The quote is apocryphal and appears in multiple variants for multitudinous uses.

25 *Myanmar Financial Sector Reforms*, World Bank, 8 July 2022, https://documents1.worldbank.org/curated/en/099950007082234868/pdf/P17700209b1e6603e0822b0be869cb8882b.pdf.

26 Microfinance was only legally established in Myanmar in 2011, via the *Microfinance Business Law* of that year.

27 For an overview of the debates over microfinance and these attributes, see David Roodman, *Due Diligence: An Inpertinant Inquiry into Microfinance,* (Washington, DC: Center for Global Development, 2012).

28 A full account of the dramas surrounding the PGMF's closure has yet to be written, but for a preliminary taste, see Eric Ellis, 'Myanmar's MFI Sector Upended by PGMF Exit', *Asiamoney,* 7 September 2023, https://www.asiamoney.com/article/2c4iv6jlwry7desxtwtts/southeast-asia/myanmars-mfi-sector-upended-by-pgmf-exit.

29 *Myanmar Financial Sector Reforms*, World Bank, 8 July 2022, https://documents1.worldbank.org/curated/en/099950007082234868/pdf/P17700209b1e6603e0822b0be869cb8882b.pdf.

30  For background on M-Pesa and its revolution, see William Cook and Claudia McKay, 'Banking in the M-PESA Age', CGAP *Working Paper*, September 2017, Consultative Group to Assist the Poor, https://www.cgap.org/research/publication/banking-m-pesa-age.

31  The opening up of Myanmar's telecommunications sector to two foreign companies (Norway's Telenor and Qatar's Ooredoo) was the most significant reform undertaken by Thein Sein's government (2011–16). So much of what that government did in terms of economic reform was superficial and tokenistic – but not this genuinely transformative initiative. The important difference: the opening of the telco sector was administered by U Winston Set Aung who would, of course, become one of the principal reformers of the NLD government too.

32  The principal author of the Master Plan was the ADB's Ian Storkey, and a tight cohort of enormously capable (mostly female) staff within Myanmar's Ministry of Planning and Finance. The UK's assistance at that time came via the Department for International Development (DfID), and as represented by some truly excellent staff at the UK Embassy in Yangon.

33  A brief overview of where we got to in opening up Myanmar's insurance sector can be found at *A Snapshot of the Myanmar Insurance Market as Local Insurers Invited to Apply for Licenses*, Tilleke and Gibbins, 29 January 2021, https://www.tilleke.com/insights/a-snapshot-of-the-myanmar-insurance-market-as-local-insurers-invited-to-apply-for-licenses/.

34  The website of the YSX is surprisingly good – both for current data, and as an authority on the bourse's history. See https://ysx-mm.com/.

35  Sean Turnell, 'A "Green" Solution to Financing Sustainable Energy in Myanmar', *Fulcrum*, 1 February 2021, ISEAS-Yusof Ishak Institute, https://fulcrum.

sg/a-green-solution-to-financing-sustainable-energy-in-myanmar/.

36  'ASEAN Green Bond Standards', *ASEAN Capital Markets Forum*, 8 March 2019, https://www.theacmf.org/initiatives/sustainable-finance/asean-green-bond-standards.

37  *Myanmar Budget Brief 2023*, The World Bank, November 2023, https://documents1.worldbank.org/curated/en/099121923041535505/pdf/P500663313e22440fe18ccf18abc281c2e1d.pdf.

38  Ibid.

39  As set out by me in a memorandum written for the State Counsellor.

40  The World Bank's 'Ease of Doing Business' survey has since been discontinued, but the past results can be found at https://www.worldbank.org/en/businessready.

41  Sean Turnell, *An Unlikely Prisoner: How an Eternal Optimist Found Hope in Myanmar's Most Notorious Jail*, (Sydney: Viking, 2023).

42  The importance of the quote and the sentiment rather exceeds that of its historical provenance – but the famous cartoon of Herbert Block in 1941 establishes its relevance in time and place. The cartoon is accessible at the website of the Library of Congress, https://www.loc.gov/pictures/item/2009632047/.

43  This conversation took place in Daw Suu's Naypyitaw residence in December 2017. I later sent a memorandum outlining similar concerns to those expressed on this day, as well as some of the options discussed in latter paragraphs here.

44  The safety of others requires a certain discretion here. For a wonderful account of some of the complexities in this

context (moral as well as practical and financial), see the memoir of the World Bank representative in Myanmar at the time: Ellen Goldstein, *Damned if You Do: Foreign Aid and My Struggle to Do Right in Myanmar*, (New York: Ballast Books, 2023).

45  See, for a general overview of Landesa as well as its work in Myanmar, https://www.landesa.org/what-we-do/asia/myanmar/.

46  I wrote and submitted the memo on 5 July 2017.

47  Jae Young Lee and Paolo Hernando, 'Electricity Reform to Light Up Myanmar's Economy', ASEAN+3 Macroeconomic Research Office (AMRO), 21 November 2019, https://amro-asia.org/electricity-reform-to-light-up-myanmars-economy/.

48  For more on such disasters, and China's coercive financial diplomacy in Southeast Asia more broadly, see Daniel O'Neill, *Dividing ASEAN and Conquering the South China Sea: China's Financial Power Projection*, (Hong Kong: Hong Kong University Press, 2018).

49  Recollection of conversation with Daw Aung San Suu Kyi, 31 July 2018, Naypyitaw, Myanmar.

50  See Nan Lwin, 'Government Spells Out Conditions for Signing BRI Deals with China', *The Irrawaddy*, 30 May 2019.

51  Yun Sun, *Slower, Smaller, Cheaper: The Reality of the China-Myanmar Economic Corridor*, Stimson Center, 26 September 2019, https://www.stimson.org/2019/slower-smaller-cheaper-reality-china-myanmar-economic-corridor/.

52  Trial documents in my possession.

53  The contract to build Myitsone was signed in late 2006 by Maung Aye (the second-ranking General in the then

ruling military regime) on the Myanmar side, and then Vice-President Xi Jinping on behalf of China. Bernard Minn, 'Dams and the Displaced: Lessons from the Myitsone Dam in Myanmar', *Global-is-Asian*, Lee Kuan Yew School of Public Policy, 20 April 2020, https://lkyspp.nus.edu.sg/gia/article/dams-and-the-displaced-lessons-from-the-myitsone-dam-in-myanmar.

54  Minn, 'Dams and the Displaced: Lessons from the Myitsone Dam in Myanmar'.

55  See Nan Lwin, 'Anti-Myitsone Campaign to Ask Citizens to Pay $1 Each to Compensate China', *The Irrawaddy,* 22 April 2019.

56  For some of the Chinese advocacy in anticipation of the NLD government's arrival in office, see Myo Lwin, 'China Hopes to Resume Myitsone Hydro Dam', *The Myanmar Times,* 9 March 2016, https://thediplomat.com/2019/03/myanmars-myitsone-dam-dilemma/.

57  In her preface to the Myanmar Economic Resilience and Reform Plan (MERRP).

58  Representative of this view; 'Why has the Pandemic Spared the Buddhist Parts of South-East Asia?', *The Economist*, 9 July 2020, https://www.economist.com/asia/2020/07/09/why-has-the-pandemic-spared-the-buddhist-parts-of-south-east-asia.

59  *Myanmar Economic Monitor, December 2020, Coping with Covid-19,* The World Bank, December 2020, https://documents1.worldbank.org/curated/en/906171608086222905/pdf/Myanmar-Economic-Monitor-Coping-with-COVID-19.pdf.

60  I provided a briefing note for the State Counsellor and her ministers on 'Modern Monetary Theory' – that alternative discourse in the economics profession that counselled

against concern over budget deficits, and which was gaining much prominence at the time. They were rightly sceptical.

61 'Myanmar Announces Covid-19 Economic Relief Plan', Tilleke and Gibbins, 7 May 2020, https://www.tilleke. com/insights/myanmar-announces-covid-19-economic-relief-plan/.

62 Data here, and all subsequent relating to CERP measures as applied, from the Ministry of Planning and Finance's unpublished 'CERP Implementation Report, October 2020'.

63 I authored the first draft of this letter.

64 For details of these arrangements under the IMF, see 'Myanmar: Requests for Disbursement Under the Rapid Credit Facility and the Rapid Financing Instrument', Statement by the Executive Director for Myanmar, 28 January 2021, https://www.imf.org/en/ Publications/CR/Issues/2021/01/25/Myanmar-Requests-for-Disbursement-Under-the-Rapid-Credit-Facility-and-Purchase-Under-the-50036.

65 Originally called the Myanmar Economic Relief and Reform Plan until, bizarrely (it seemed to Myanmar's reformers), the IMF objected to the word 'relief'. We gathered that the Fund thought this label was attached to measures that were purely for short-term amelioration, and therefore outside the scope of the facilities on offer.

66 Nehginpao Kipgen, 'The 2020 Myanmar Election and the 2021 Coup', *Asian Affairs,* Vol.52, No.1, 2021, https://www.tandfonline.com/doi/abs/10.1080/0306837 4.2021.1886429.

67 Data on Covid has been actively suppressed by the SAC junta, but the following gives a taste of the catastrophe: 'The COVID-19 Third Wave in Myanmar Following

the Military Coup', National Library of Medicine, US National Center for Biotechnology Information, 22 June 2023, https://pubmed.ncbi.nlm.nih.gov/37841829/.

68 'Import Requirements and Documentation', *Burma, Country Commercial Guide*, International Trade Commission, US Department of Commerce, https://www.trade.gov/country-commercial-guides/burma-import-requirements-and-documentation.

69 Khine Lin Kyaw, 'Myanmar Asks for Suspension of Foreign Loan Payments', Bloomberg, 14 July 2022, https://www.bnnbloomberg.ca/myanmar-asks-for-suspension-of-foreign-loan-payments-1.1792197.

70 World Bank, *Myanmar Economic Monitor*, December 2023, https://documents1.worldbank.org/curated/en/099121112308208497 1/pdf/P5006630739fd70a00a66coe15bf7b34917.pdf.

71 Ye Myo Hein, 'Myanmar's Fateful Conscription Law', United States Institute of Peace, 26 February 2024, https://www.usip.org/publications/2024/02/myanmars-fateful-conscription-law.

72 Ibid.

73 A detailed analysis of the collapse of the *kyat* in the wake of the coup is contained in the World Bank's January 2023 edition of its *Myanmar Economic Monitor,* https://documents1.worldbank.org/curated/en/099134001292342538/pdf/P1791060704c4d0720a7acoc3c23f1b5b90.pdf.

74 'Myanmar's Garment Industry has Shrunk by 25% Since the Military Coup', *TEXtalks,* 6 February 2024, https://textalks.com/myanmars-garment-industry-has-shrunk-by-25-since-the-military-coup/.

75 World Bank, *Myanmar Economic Monitor*, December 2023.

76  Guillaume De Langre, 'The End of Myanmar's Resource Boom Could Doom the Junta', *Frontier,* 19 December 2023, https://www.frontiermyanmar.net/en/the-end-of-myanmars-resource-boom-could-doom-the-junta/.

77  *Myanmar Microfinance Sector Evolution, MFI Health Check Survey Results Phase II*, Myanmar Microfinance Association, November 2022, https://www.rfilc.org/wp-content/uploads/2023/06/Myanmar-Microfinance-Sector-Evolution-MFI-Health-Check-Survey-Results.pdf.

78  World Bank, *Myanmar Economic Monitor*, December 2023, https://documents1.worldbank.org/curated/en/099121123082084971/pdf/P5006630739fd70a00a66c0e15bf7b34917.pdf.

79  PGMF staff reported to me, on numerous occasions, instances of intimidation from Myanmar's military and from the Department of Cooperatives (within the Ministry of Agriculture) and of threats of a forced takeover of their operations.

80  Hein Htoo Zan, 'Myanmar Junta Drives Largest Micro Lender Out of Business', *The Irrawaddy,* 27 June 2023.

81  'Junta Weaponises Digital Banking Transition to Starve Resistance Funding', *Frontier,* 7 October 2022, https://www.frontiermyanmar.net/en/junta-weaponises-digital-banking-transition-to-starve-resistance-funding%EF%BF%BC/.

82  For a thorough account of Telenor's withdrawal, and its implications, see Thompson Chau, 'Myanmar Military Approves Norwegian Telenor's Exit', *Nikkei Asia,* 18 March 2022, https://asia.nikkei.com/Business/Telecommunication/Myanmar-military-approves-Norwegian-Telenor-s-exit.

83  'KBZ Users Struggle Under Junta Surveillance', *Frontier,* 28 April 2023, https://www.frontiermyanmar.net/en/kbz-users-struggle-under-junta-surveillance/.

84  *Policing Mobile Money: Digital Financial Repression in Post-Coup Myanmar*, Knowledge for Democracy Myanmar, International Development Research Centre (Canada), January 2024, https://k4dm.ca/wp-content/uploads/2024/04/K4DM-MDR-02-Policing-Mobile-Money.pdf.

85  In my 2009 book, *Fiery Dragons,* I give a long and detailed examination of the role of *hundi* in Myanmar. Sean Turnell, *Fiery Dragons*, (Copenhagen: NIAS Press, 2009).

86  'Money is coined liberty' – the phrase, repeated often in libertarian monetary circles, has its origins in Fyodor Dostoyevsky's *The House of the Dead* (London: J.M. Dent, 1911).

87  For a complete overview of all the international sanctions applying to Myanmar, see Maya Lester and Michael O'Kane, 'Burma/Myanmar Sanctions Regime', *Global Sanctions*, accessed 27 March 2024, https://globalsanctions.co.uk/region/burma/.

88  'Myanmar Delisted from EITI Due to Political Instability', Extractive Industries Transparency Initiative, 29 February 2024, https://eiti.org/news/myanmar-delisted-eiti-due-political-instability.

89  'Major Opium Economy Expansion is Underway in Myanmar', United Nations Office on Drugs and Crime (UNODC), 26 January 2023, https://www.unodc.org/roseap/en/myanmar/2023/01/myanmar-opium-survey-report/story.html.

90  See, as one excellent report among many from USIP, Priscilla Clapp and Jason Tower, 'A Criminal Cancer Spreads in Southeast Asia', 26 June 2023, https://www.usip.org/publications?experts[0]=133121&page=1.

91  Comprising the Arakan Army, Myanmar National Democratic Alliance Army, Ta'ang National Liberation Army.

92  For an introduction to some of these instruments, see
    International Crisis Group, *Crowdfunding a War: The
    Money Behind Myanmar's Resistance,* 20 December
    2022, https://icg-prod.s3.amazonaws.com/s3fs-public/
    2022-12/328-myanmars-resistance.pdf.

# Lowy Institute Penguin Specials

# MODERN WARFARE

Sir Lawrence Freedman

A LOWY INSTITUTE PAPER

More than any other modern war, the fight between Russia and Ukraine has been a tough testing ground for modern weapons and operational concepts.

Drawing on extensive research into the conduct of the war during its first year, Sir Lawrence Freedman assesses the contrasting strategies of the two sides. Ukraine has fought along classical lines, seeking victory through battle. Russia has adopted a more total approach, combining conventional battles with attacks on Ukraine's socio-economic structure. Freedman explains why the apparently superior Russian force has been unable to defeat and subjugate Ukraine.

PENGUIN
SPECIALS

# RISE OF THE EXTREME RIGHT

## Lydia Khalil

A LOWY INSTITUTE PAPER

ASIO says right-wing extremism now makes up half its case load, and that it anticipates a terrorist attack on Australian soil within the year. There has been a 250 per cent increase in right-wing terrorism globally. So what exactly is right-wing extremism and how is its potential for violence growing? Why is it a global problem? How does it threaten democracy and what should we do about it? *Rise of the Extreme Right* answers these questions while situating Australia within the global threat landscape.

# Powered by Penguin

**Looking for more great reads, exclusive content and book giveaways?**
Subscribe to our weekly newsletter.

Scan the QR code or visit penguin.com.au/signup